W hen James Prosek was just fifteen, a ranger named Joe Haines caught him fishing without a permit in a stream near his home in Connecticut. But instead of trying to escape like his fishing buddy, James put down his rod and surrendered. It was a move that would change his life forever. Expecting a small fine and a lecture, James instead received enough knowledge about fishing and the great outdoors to last a lifetime.

The story of this unlikely friendship between two men—one old, one young—*Joe and Me* captures both the enthusiasm of youth and the wisdom of experience. As Joe passes on his affection for nature to his eager student, James's reflections are, in turn, intimate and expansive, inspirational and full of wonder.

From a talent *The New York Times* calls "a fair bid to become the Audubon of the fishing world," comes a book that every lover of the outdoors will cherish: a journal about fishing, the spirit of nature, and that one mentor in a young man's life who changes the way he looks at the world.

JOE AND ME

ALSO BY JAMES PROSEK

Trout: An Illustrated History

JOE AND ME

*An Education
in Fishing and Friendship*

James Prosek

ROB WEISBACH BOOKS
William Morrow and Company, Inc. New York

The people and places in this book are real, and I am thankful to have lived among them. Joe Haines continues to teach me things. I extend thanks to my sister, Jennifer Prosek, and to Elaine Markson. I am grateful to Colin Dickerman and Rob Weisbach, for their insight, energy, and vision.

Published by Rob Weisbach Books
An Imprint of William Morrow and Company, Inc.
1350 Avenue of the Americas, New York, N.Y. 10019

It is the policy of William Morrow and Company, Inc., and its imprints and affiliates, recognizing the importance of preserving what has been written, to print the books we publish on acid-free paper, and we exert our best efforts to that end.

Library of Congress Cataloging-in-Publication Data

Prosek, James, 1975–
    Joe and me : an education in fishing and friendship / James
Prosek.—1st ed.
        p.   cm.
    ISBN 0-688-15316-X (hardcover)
    1. Prosek, James, 1975–   2. Haines, Joe, 1937–
3. Fishers—United States—Biography.   I. Title.
SH415.P76A3   1997
799.1'092—dc21   97-10039
                                                            CIP

Printed in the United States of America

First Edition

1   2   3   4   5   6   7   8   9   10   3 2901 00175 9035

INTERIOR DESIGN BY LEAH S. CARLSON
COVER DESIGN BY BRADFORD FOLTZ
COVER ILLUSTRATION BY JAMES PROSEK

CONTENTS

Caught   *1*

Taunton Lake   *13*

First Striper   *23*

Blue Crabs   *35*

Clover   *47*

The Drowned Boy   *55*

On Patrol   *67*

Salmon River   *77*

Wolf Pit 93

Brutus 103

Pheasant 115

Lead 125

Sherwood Island 133

Ice Fishing 143

Candlewood Lake 155

Equinox 165

Orchard 173

The Gift 183

JOE AND ME

Sign posted at the Aspetuck Reservoir

CAUGHT

It's not like I had never done it before. In fact, poaching had almost become an art to me. I prided myself on being discreet and having successfully evaded the law for years. The Easton Reservoir, owned by the Bridgeport Hydraulic Company, is just a short walk from my home, and it was where I spent most afternoons fishing. Along with the Aspetuck and Saugatuck reservoirs, Easton was routinely patrolled by wardens whose job it was to keep anyone who was a threat to water quality off the property. That apparently meant anyone who even went near it.

At fifteen, the thought of getting caught breaking the law was both frightening and exhilarating. I was well aware of the danger of fishing illegally, and although I'd never been caught, I had mapped out every possible means of escape. Stone foundations, left from when the water company tore down old houses, would make ideal hiding places. The stone walls that crisscrossed the woods, remnants of farmers' attempts to rid the soil of rocks and keep their cows fenced in, would be good for ducking behind at the last minute. Large sycamores and sugar maples with low branches would be ideal for climbing if I felt that the best way to escape was up. I had found or cut trails in every direction, sought out undercut banks where I could crawl if I was trapped against the water, and even entertained the idea of swimming to the other side of the reservoir or to one of the two small islands in the middle if there was no alternative. But the danger of getting caught was only part of the attraction of fishing where I did. More than the thrill, it was the prospect of catching a large trout that kept me going back, and that same prospect led me from the familiar Easton Reservoir to the Aspetuck, where I found myself one afternoon standing on the lip of the dam, next to my friend Stephen, in the pouring rain.

We had run with our equipment through the woods, our ponchos trailing behind us like great green capes in the heavy April rain. Exposed to the road and bordered by a swamp, the dam was undoubtedly the worst possible place a poacher could find himself. I hesitated before moving into the open, crouching against the wind to tie a lure on my line. My hands were shaking, from the cold or nerves or both, but I managed to tie the knot and climbed onto the dam to cast. I whipped the rod in a wide arc, but the line blew back and landed at my feet. I cast again but had no luck. Frustrated with the conditions and feeling exposed, I hid behind a concrete pump house that was perched on the rim of the dam, trying to keep an eye on the road. Stephen persisted in attempting to cast his line into the reservoir.

"This is crazy, Stephen!" I yelled through the downpour. "We're not going to catch anything. Let's wait in the woods till your mom comes back to pick us up."

He couldn't hear me.

My eyes tried to focus on the road, which I could barely make out through the sheets of rain. A blue wash of color appeared, heading our way, and I somehow knew it was a warden's patrol truck. As it approached, I froze behind the pump house, unable to move. Moments later, the blue truck pulled up behind us. Its tires on the gravel were, incredibly, even louder than the rain.

I yelled to Stephen, who had already seen the truck, and we ran down the hill to the edge of the swamp. Stephen jumped in without hesitation and started to cross, his rod in his teeth, the stagnant water up past his hips.

He removed his rod long enough to scream, "Come on!" but I didn't follow.

I turned around and looked up the hill that we had just come down. Standing at the top was a man in silhouette, briefly illuminated by a faint spark that appeared below the peak of his hunting cap. He had lit a cigarette.

I stood looking at him, the rain running off my poncho, and watched as a plume of smoke disappeared over his shoulder. The odds of my escape seemed slight. If I had been at the edge of a broad expanse of woodland I might have considered running. But I was trapped, the swamp on one side, the warden on the other, and beyond, roads most certainly now being patrolled by backup in search of any young boy carrying a fishing rod.

I put down my head and trudged up the hill, the water sloshing in my shoes, the rain dripping from my hair. I walked right up to him.

"I know who you are, James," the man said, squinting his eyes. I was surprised he knew my name and was overcome by the feeling that he had watched me before, that he had saved my capture for this day. Why hadn't I been caught earlier? I had fished the reservoir behind my house every single summer day for years. He must have seen me there. Had he *let* me poach all these years? Maybe I wasn't as discreet as I had thought.

I knew who he was too, though, and I had watched *him* on occasion. His name was Joe Haines. I remembered one July day seeing him help bale hay in Farmer Kaechele's field. My father had told me he was a patrolman, and was married to Kaechele's daughter. And now I was standing before him, caught.

"Let's get out of the rain," he said. "Put your gear in the back of the pickup truck."

"You think you could drive me home?" I asked abruptly, hoping to solve the problem of what to do with me. The thought had crossed my mind that I could go to jail. There was a silence while I waited for his verdict. Would he fine me? Just scold me? I braced myself. Instead, he just changed the subject.

"We need to find your friend before we head back," he said. I put my rod and box of lures in the back of his truck and pulled a green tarpaulin over them, securing the edge with a deer antler that was sitting in the flatbed. Before we stepped in, I noticed

Haines eyeing my boots. Though I had been careful over the years not to leave obvious marks of my passing, even an animal moving across the forest floor leaves tracks. I suspected that mine were familiar to Haines, but he was silent. He climbed into the cab and I did the same, slamming the heavy door against the weather.

"What's your friend's name?" Haines asked.

Stephen and I had always said that we would use aliases if one of us got caught. But I had never anticipated that the patrolman who caught me would already know *my* name. Lying seemed out of the question. "His name is Stephen."

I had hidden from blue patrol trucks just like this one all my life, and I honestly never thought I'd be in one. It wasn't too clean inside the cab, but it was warm, and I immediately thought of how cold Stephen must be. On the seat between us was a stack of papers and catalogs full of fishing equipment. The CB radio sputtered, and Haines picked it up.

"You there, Csanadi?"

"Yeah."

He continued talking into the receiver with his thumb firmly pressed on the black button. I knew he was talking with the police because I went to school with Officer Csanadi's son. As he spoke, looking out through the windshield into the rain, I watched him. He was an older, white-haired man, obviously weathered from a lifetime of exposure to the elements. His hands were worn. They reminded me of old farmers' hands I'd seen, soil trapped under the fingernails.

"We got one but the other is through the swamp," Haines

said. He released his thumb from the button and looked at me. "Is that right?" he asked. "Did Stephen go through the swamp?"

"Yeah. Stephen doesn't think too much, he just kind of reacts."

"Well, you were smart not to run." He picked up the receiver and spoke into it. "We might want to get out the fire department to look for the kid. Name's Stephen."

"We're doing our best on this end," Officer Csanadi's voice crackled through the static.

I shivered, still uncertain what Haines had in mind for me. Would they publish my crime in the town paper? What would my father say when I got home?

Minutes later, we heard the news that a policeman had found Stephen huddled in the dugout of the baseball field across the street from the swamp. I had to give him credit for trying.

Haines and I drove out from the dam and turned onto the road toward home. Looking again at the catalogs between us on the seat of the cab, I asked him if he liked to fish.

"I like to fish," he said. "But I fish legally. I know your parents split up and all, but that's no reason to go out and break the law. You can catch just as many fish in legal waters. What were you expecting to catch there, anyway?"

My parents had split up five years ago, when I was ten. It was strange to hear such personal information about my family coming from a man I didn't know.

"Stephen said he caught an eighteen-inch brook trout off the dam yesterday. He said they were wild fish. I was tempted. Usually I'm not stupid enough to fish off a dam."

"Wild trout, eighteen inches?" Haines snorted with disbelief.

"Why, aren't there trout in the Aspetuck?"

"Well, none eighteen inches, that's for sure." He noticed the camera I had around my neck, which I had been careful to keep dry. "Do you take pictures of the fish you catch?"

"I take a picture of them and then let them go."

"When I go fishing I usually don't let them go. I'm fishing for the pot. I go fishing to fill my belly. Don't you like to eat fish?"

"Of course I do."

We drove on a bit more in silence until Haines said, "We'll stop by my house on the way." I knew then this stern law enforcer had taken it upon himself to turn me around from what he saw as a life of crime.

His red colonial house, on Old Oak Road, was nestled in a terraced lawn and dwarfed by the swooping arcs of ancient sugar maples. I had passed it every day on the school bus. On especially cold mornings, when light was just breaking the darkness, blue-gray smoke spiraled from the chimney.

He parked in the gravel driveway and we walked through the doors to the inside of his small home. We were greeted by the warmth of the woodstove.

"I cranked it up to take the chill off," he said, opening the latch and pitching in another log. It seemed I had turned from criminal to welcome houseguest in a matter of minutes.

The knotty-pine boards on the walls made me feel like I was in the heart of a great tree. Rough-hewn beams stretched across the ceiling, holding up the second floor. I felt that I had been in this house before, smelled the wood smoke, and heard the floorboards creaking with my step. It felt like home.

A shaggy white and brown dog ran around the corner of the living room and up to Haines.

"Hey, Nella," he said, patting her on the head absent-mindedly. She then came over to me, whining softly. I gave her a scratch behind the ears as I looked around.

On the mantel I saw a black-and-white picture of Haines in his youth, holding a fox by the tail. He was now, I guessed, in his mid-fifties. Next to the photograph were several quartz arrowheads and an old Currier & Ives print of two fishermen by a stream. The beautiful scene it captured was nothing like the storm we had just escaped.

It became clear after a quick glance around his house that Haines did not fish *only* for the pot. He was a sportsman, too—stuffed fish hung on almost every wall. He saw me looking at one fish mounted above the bookshelves; it was yellow, with black vertical stripes and bright orange fins.

"That one there is from Candlewood Lake," he said.

"It's huge! Is that a perch?" I asked. I had never seen one so big.

"Yeah, we get them like that ice fishing, call 'em humpbacks 'cause of that huge hump they got. I've got them even bigger than that before."

He invited me upstairs to see where he tied flies for fly-fishing. The stairs were steep and I had to duck not to hit my head on the ceiling.

"That's a huge fish," I said, looking at one mounted above his desk.

"That's a king."

"King salmon?"

"Yeah, from the Salmon River in Pulaski, New York. And this"—he lifted a black bundle with a hook on it from a pile of feather clippings—"is the killer fly. Do you fly-fish at all?"

"You bet. A bit too windy today for it," I said, trying to make a joke. He didn't reply.

"Well, maybe soon I'll get you out to do a bit of trout fishing. But right now, I should get you home."

"That'd be great."

He turned to look at me, suddenly more serious than before. "James, I'm not going to fine you; I'm going to give you a written warning. Everyone deserves a second chance. You can fish the reservoirs all you want, but next time you're caught you'll be arrested."

On the way home, as we rode in silence, I examined the floor of the cab, trying to learn something more about Haines. There was an empty carton of Salem cigarettes, an old rusted spinning lure, leaves and wood chips, a clipboard for daily reports, a pair of binoculars, a shotgun shell, a turkey wing feather and a pheasant tail feather, a tin of Copenhagen, and a single badly stained work glove—all strewn about haphazardly. The cab smelled like wet bark.

"I think I saw you once," I said, breaking the stillness of the cab, "baling hay in Kaechele's field."

"Yeah, I helped old Kaechele out from time to time. He was my father-in-law, but just as stubborn as all those old farmers, can't get them to do anything if it's not the way they've always done it. I helped him cut wood once. He'd cut the trees in ten-foot sections, then cart them to his garden behind the house. Then he'd bring out this saw attachment for his tractor and cut the logs in three-foot pieces for the woodstove. Had to use that old saw just 'cause he had it. Then he'd split the wood with an ax and pile it thirty yards from the house. I told him, I said, 'Let me use my chain saw and I'll cut the tree into three-foot segments on the spot. Then I'll split it with a maul, and then stack it on your back doorstep.' He'd never let me, and so I stopped helping him, because we always had to do it his way."

Haines pulled into my driveway. It was strange that we lived only five minutes from each other but had never met until that day. "Well," he said as I opened the door to get out, "I'll give you a call to go fishing. And I'm gonna show you that you can catch just as many fish in legal waters. All's you have to do," he said to me, "is learn how to look. There's a lot of fish out there that no one catches and there's a lot of fishermen who just aren't willing to put in the time. There's a lot of fishermen who think they know everything, but the best ones I know admit that they can never know it all."

I did not have to prove my love of fishing to Haines; he had caught me in the act on the most miserable day of the year. I had been soaked from head to toe, but even so, I could sense somehow that Haines wished he, too, had been out fishing in the rain. There was a look in his eyes that told me he, too, had also once been a poacher, and a damn good one. After all, who better to catch a poacher than one who had reformed?

Trolling with lead core line

TAUNTON LAKE

Haines kept his promise to take me fishing. I hadn't thought he was going to call, but he did, one Saturday afternoon. The initial invitation was a bit awkward for both of us.

"I like to take the kids I catch fishing," he said to me over the phone, "to show them that there are just as many fish in legal waters."

Something about his tone of voice told me that Haines wasn't exactly telling the truth. I doubted he made a habit out of taking kids he had caught fishing, but he wasn't sure how to ask me, so he made it sound like part of his job.

He said he was taking me to a private lake in Newtown called Taunton. Coming to pick me up in an hour, if that was okay. It was. As we drove, he commented on the things we passed; he knew the owner of Swanson's Fish Market, had pruned trees every spring at Slady's Farm, and had bought lumber at Henderson's. From the moment he picked me up at my house

---

in his old black Chevy truck, I began to see things through his eyes.

By the upper reaches of the Pequonnuck River, where I had fished many times before, Haines spotted a large snapping turtle crossing the road.

"Hold on a minute," he said, pulling off to the side and getting out of the truck. I followed him out, leaping from the Chevy's high platform.

"Don't want it to get hit," he said, grabbing the turtle by the tail and holding it out from his body so that its long neck and jaws couldn't reach his leg. He moved it to safety, and I watched the turtle waddle off into the damp swampy woods.

"Would have kept it to eat," Haines said, once we were back in the truck.

"What, the turtle?" I asked him. "You eat turtles?"

"Sure, but my freezer's packed with meat as it is. I got some heavy eating to do." He cleared his throat.

"How would you eat a turtle?" I asked Haines. "Are they any good?"

"Snappers have got sweet meat. I've got some friends that love 'em. I usually bring 'em to Danny Lee or Earl, and they prepare 'em and bring me a container with turtle soup. You could make a lot of soup from a turtle the size we just saw."

"How big would you say that turtle was?"

"Oh geez, that one'd go probably forty pounds. Lots of meat on that one. I've cleaned them myself before but it takes a lot of work."

"What do you have to do?" I asked. I had already figured out that the best way to keep a conversation going with Haines was to ask him questions, and sitting in silence with him still made me a bit nervous.

"Well, some'll shoot off the head with a shotgun, or take a pitchfork and put it through their head to stretch the neck out, and then chop off the head with a hatchet. Then you got to hang the turtle by the tail on a tree and let it bleed out a good, long time. You can take that turtle off the tree in two days, lay it on the ground, and it'll still walk around."

"Are you serious? With its head cut off for two days?" I had trouble believing it, but couldn't help picturing the gruesome scene in my head.

"Yeah, it takes them about four days to die, their heart beats so slow. They got a real slow metabolism."

At the flagpole in Newtown, just past the police station, we took a left and drove down a long, steep hill. We came to the lake and circled around part of it, and then drove up a road to a steep sloping lawn with a small, plain brown clapboard house perched on it. There was a dock in the distance, with one lone white pine in front of it.

The lake was flat, except for occasional ripples as fish broke the surface. I could picture the lake coming alive with feeding trout. Haines started carrying equipment down the hill to the dock and I followed him. On the second trip, I asked if he wanted me to carry the battery, but he had already grabbed it and was straining down the hill with it. I followed with his tackle box in a white bucket and the electric trolling motor.

The lawn was soggy and smelled like spring. "This house belongs to my friend Red Wagner," Haines said

"He like to fish?" I asked.

"Yeah, but he don't get out as much as he used to. He's fading a bit, getting old."

I followed Haines to the edge of the property, where there was an aluminum boat up on wooden sawhorses. We lifted it, turned it right side up, and carried it down the sloping lawn, sliding it into the water. Taking the bowline, Haines led the boat to the dock and tied it up, and we filled it with our gear. He walked to a nearby shed and pulled out his key chain, which must have had thirty keys on it. He released the padlock and then swung open the door. Inside, we grabbed two seat cushions, a pair of oars, and two orange badges with pins.

"This is a backpatch," he said, holding a piece of orange paper, "which says you're a guest at the Newtown Fish and Game Club. You can thank old Red for that when you meet him." Now I was legal, I thought, and somehow, a new member of the club. After all, he wanted to introduce me to his old friend. I had been wondering if this was a one-time thing, but it seemed that Haines already had plans to take me fishing again.

We got in the aluminum boat and pushed off. Haines clamped his small electric trolling motor to the stern and then rowed us out.

"Oh," he said as he was putting his two-piece fishing rod together, "I met your friend Stephen's mother the other day at Greiser's store. Boy, is she proud of her son. She said to me, 'You won't catch my Stephen again; he can sprint like a deer and swim like an otter.'"

I couldn't help but laugh; this was typical of her. Haines continued, "And I said to her, 'Ma'am, your Stephen can swim, but he's got to come to the other side at some point.' She shut up for a while, and then she insisted that she was my classmate down in Bridgeport, but I never went to the school she was talking about." He dipped the oar in the water and stroked and then stopped to hook up the trolling motor to the battery.

"Stephen's mom means well," I said. "When did she think she knew you?" Haines strung the line through his guides and selected a fly.

"I guess grammar school. I never liked school that much," Haines said. "I had to make money, my teachers never understood that. Trapping was how I made most of my money as a kid."

"What kind of stuff did you trap?"

"Muskrat mostly. Occasionally I'd get a mink and get a load of money for it. Trapped a few fox. But the competition started getting stiff, guys were overlapping my territory, and eventually I stopped. There were very few houses north of your house in the Tashua area back then. I could walk through the woods from my house to the Merritt Parkway and hunt squirrels all day. I had it all to myself."

I watched Haines rig up his rod.

"Ever use lead-core line?" he asked, holding up the rod.

"No."

"Well, the line is heavy and it gets the fly down if the fish are deep." He tied the fly to the line and laid it in the water. Starting the engine again, he let out about thirty feet of line. "Why don't you get out your fly rod and tie on something about two inches long," Haines said. I put a fly on my line and let out as much line as he had. "Your line should be closer to the surface than mine," he said. "That way we can cover more water."

Haines put his rod in a holder by the edge of the boat so he could steer the engine. It was the first time this year I'd noticed the sun was getting higher in the sky. The shadows were strong. We'd trolled about three hundred yards before anything happened.

"I think I had a bite," I said, holding my fly rod in my hand.

"Does it feel like a good fish?" Haines asked.

"I can't tell," I said, and then I felt it jerk again. "There he is again."

"He gave you a second chance."

"Yeah, he's on now." I reeled the fish up to the boat with ease. It wasn't a trout, which is what I was expecting. It was a largemouth bass.

"Mudsucker," Haines said as he netted it.

"Mudsucker?"

"Yeah, them bass aren't good for anything. People go nuts over 'em but I don't see what the big deal is; they make one effort to fight, then they give up. And if you eat them in the summer they taste like mud. The only time of year they're any good to eat is in winter, when you catch them through the ice and their flesh is good and firm."

"Bass are what I mostly fished for all my life," I said to Haines. "I think they fight well."

"Well, they don't fight like a trout, and they don't taste near as good. Oop, there's one," he said, hooking a fish and reeling in his line. I let the bass go and then netted his fish, a lovely little yellow perch with bright orange lower fins, a yellow-green body, and dark vertical bands along its sides.

"Barred trout," Haines said.

"Barred trout? Don't you mean yellow perch?" I asked him.

"Barred trout are better than bass. They've got real nice white meat that flakes off when you cook it. This one's too small," Haines said, tossing it back into the dark water.

"That was a perch," I said to Haines, trying one more time, "right?"

"Barred trout," he said.

"O.K.," I murmured. I soon learned that Haines had his own particular way of naming things.

"That fish must have gone, oh, six, maybe eight pounds . . . I mean inches," Haines said, laughing, and I saw a playful side of him I hadn't yet seen. He began to rummage through the white bucket where he kept all his equipment. Pulling out a fly box, he opened it, picked out a fly, and handed it to me.

"Here."

"What kind of fly is this?" I asked.

"It's top secret. Don't even hold it out over the water or a trout will jump out and take it," he said, smiling. "It's a Joe Haines Special. Do you tie any flies?" he asked.

"Yeah, I've been tying since I was eight," I said and turned the buggy black fly in my hand. "How do you make it?"

"I tie on the black marabou tail first," Haines said. "Then I wrap the hook with lead, 'cause you got to get it down there if you want to catch anything. Then I take about a foot-long segment of black wool and divide it into four strands. Take one of the strands and tie it in the front part of the hook. Start wrapping it back and then wrap it over itself again. You got it so far?"

"Yeah, sounds a lot like a woolly bugger," I said, referring to a popular fly.

"Just wait till I finish, James. You got it in your hand, you

---

19

can see it's not just a woolly bugger." He paused to remember where he'd left off. "Then tie in the gray hackle in the front and, bringing the thread to the back, wind the feather to the rear and tie it off. Now, here's the part that counts," he said, pointing to the fly in my hand. "See that marabou collar that runs on top of the fly in a half-moon?"

"Yeah."

"Well, you make it by tying in three pieces of marabou, one on one side, one on the other, and one on top, and then clip them down even, to about a quarter inch long. Now, when that collar gets wet," Haines said, taking the fly back out of my hand and dunking it in the lake, "it looks just like the shell on the top of a hellgrammite, see?" I leaned over the side of the boat to look. "And the last thing I like to do is trim the hackle so that it's kind of rough and spindly. It looks more like little legs that way. I'm telling you, when nothing else is working, this will. That's all there is to it. Just don't go telling everyone 'cause then there won't be any fish left for us."

"Can I keep it?" I asked Haines.

"Use it as a model," he said to me. "It's yours."

"Then let me give you a fly," I said and pulled out a small Adams dry fly that I had tied and handed it to him.

"You tied this?" Haines said, examining it between his fingers.

"Yes."

"I could never tie anything this small, my hands aren't steady enough." I was flattered that Haines acknowledged my skill. It gave me the confidence to fish with him, someone who'd been around a long time.

We let our lines out again until we swung around to Red Wagner's dock, where we had started. We cast for another hour in the cove by the dock and Haines caught a larger perch and put it in the bucket.

"You always keep the fish you catch?" I asked him.

"I never keep more than my limit, James. It amazes me how greedy people can be." He cast and began to retrieve his fly. "One day my son Joey and this doctor friend of mine were out fishing on Taunton. Joey was young then, maybe eight or nine. The doctor caught his legal limit, five fish, and when he caught a sixth he threw it in the bucket with the minnows. Joey didn't say anything to the doctor, but he told me when he came home. I'd had other problems with this guy too; all he'd do was take take take, never gave anything back. Greedy. This last thing topped it off for me. You gonna just take like that, that's not friendship." From the tone of Haines's voice, I knew at some point he'd been good friends with the doctor. He didn't say what happened, but I assumed things had changed. Haines took another cast.

We fished a bit longer, and when the light grew dim, Haines rowed us back to the dock.

"Sorry we didn't get any trout," he said, laying one of the oars on the dock.

"No, that's all right, I had a great time."

"Well, we'll have to get you out again," he said. I helped unload the equipment, watching the sky grow dark around us, hoping he would stick to his word.

Striped Bass caught off Southport Beach

FIRST STRIPER

A few weeks later, around noon, Haines pulled into my driveway in his blue patrol truck. Seeing it through the window, I felt as though I'd done something illegal, the same feeling I get when I see a police car. I went out to say hello. Haines let the truck idle for a minute as he pulled up the parking brake. He stayed in the truck, talking through the open window.

"Can't stay long, James. Just wanted to tell you it's a good tide tonight for fishing off the beach. I know you've been asking about striper fishing. Do you want to go?"

"Yeah," I said.

"Let's see, low tide is at eight so we should be getting off at about seven. You ever cast off the beach?"

"No, but I used to fish in the sound, off my uncle's boat, for blues."

"Well, if we go tonight, sounds like you'll get a taste of something new. Fishing off a beach is different than off a boat," he said.

23

"So I'll need my waders?"

"I think you will, unless you want to go in with a bathing suit. What have you got for a rod?"

"About an eight-foot rod with a Penn reel on it, one of the old gold ones."

"A spinning reel?" he asked.

"Yeah," I said. "Do you want to come in and see it?"

"I should stay by the truck in case I get a call on the radio. I'm not off duty till four-thirty. Bring it out and we'll take a look."

Haines shut off the engine and stepped out of his truck onto the lawn. I ran inside to get the rod.

"Feels pretty good," he said, "good action but a bit too light for the kind of fish we're after. Bob Gost will probably lend you one."

I didn't ask who Bob Gost was but I assumed he was coming fishing with us. Haines had a way of talking about people without bothering to tell me who they were. Instead of bothering me, it made me feel instantly like I was becoming part of his world.

"Why don't you get a weight to tie on to the line," Haines said, "and we'll cast it a bit. The line you got on here looks old. If you hook a big bass you want everything to be right, 'cause there's a lot that can go wrong."

I handed Haines about a half-ounce weight and he tied it on. He cast on my front lawn. The line flew out about twenty feet and then stopped, recoiling at our feet.

"You're gonna need some new line," he said, handing me the rod. "Why don't you come over at about six-thirty; you can have a bite to eat. We'll put some new line on your reel and get down to the beach for the low tide."

From my closet where I keep all my fishing gear, I pulled out an old vest and decided it would become my saltwater vest. I didn't have any saltwater fishing tackle, but my father had some. He kept it in a cabinet in the laundry room, and because he rarely fished, I considered all the tackle he had to be mine. Removing his stainless-steel hooks and large plugs and spoons, I stuffed them in the pockets of the vest to prepare for the evening.

I had had my driver's license for only six days, and I thought of it as a new fishing tool, granting me access to streams and lakes all over the state. Loading up my rod, vest, and waders, I sped over to Haines's for dinner. By now, we'd been fishing several times, and I was begining to feel more comfortable around him.

"Got all your stuff?" he said as soon as I'd pulled in.

"Yeah, I've got all I have."

"Well, why don't you take out your rod so we can respool it later." He took it and leaned it against the house. We went inside. A woman with red hair, slightly graying, was sitting at the round table in the kitchen, looking through a seed catalog. "Muriel, this is James. James, this is my wife, Muriel."

"You going fishing with Joe?" she asked.

"Yeah, I guess we're going to fish the beach for stripers."

I suppose she knew I was the boy Haines had caught, but she didn't say anything about it. She didn't ask when we were going to be back, but simply got up and said, "I'm going to go weed the flower garden, Joe. James, it was nice to meet you. You guys have a good time."

When she had left, I picked up the seed catalog and flipped through it.

"How's a roast beef sandwich sound? I've got fresh Portuguese rolls."

"Sounds great."

"I like to put on a slice of cheese and tomato and then melt it. I'll chop up some hot peppers too. You like hot peppers?"

"Depends how hot," I said.

"They're pretty mild, but they add a lot to a sandwich. Cherry soda okay?"

"Yeah, thanks."

"I gave a call to Bob Gost. He's gonna come along with us tonight."

"What's he like?"

"Bobber's got a heart of gold," Haines said, putting my can of soda and a glass down on the table in front of me. I pushed the seed catalog aside.

"Why do you call him Bobber?" I asked.

" 'Cause he's round like a fishing bobber. Big guy, 'bout three hundred pounds—well, maybe not that big. When we go ice fishing, we send him out first to test the ice. I figure, if he doesn't go through, it's safe. Just don't go near him when he eats pickled eggs," Haines laughed. "There's not a kinder man on the earth. I need help and he's right there. A thing you'll learn, James, you take care of someone and they'll take care of you."

Despite his joking, I could tell Haines was serious about his friendships.

Bob Gost rolled into the driveway and hopped out of his truck. He was stocky, and his wide smile was framed by a rusty brown beard. "I've heard a lot about you," he said as he shook my hand and grinned. "The old man is very fond of you already." Haines walked inside to get some fishing line to spool my reel with. "There aren't many people he speaks highly of. It's very nice to meet you."

"It's nice to meet you, too." It was strange to hear that Haines was saying good things about me, or even talking about me at all.

"Do you have an extra rod for James?" Haines asked Bob.

"I think I do in the back of the truck," he said. "Why, is his too light?"

"Yeah, it would break in half. If he hooks into a big striper I want him to have a rod with some backbone. We'll have James use one of your rods and the Penn reel he's got here; I'm spooling it with twelve pound test line." He looked at me. "James, take the old line off your reel so we can put new stuff on." When I'd stripped off the old line, Haines tied on the line from a new spool and wound it on my reel.

"New moon tonight," Bob said.

"Is that good?" I asked.

"The new moon is the best for big stripers," Haines said.

"How big have you got them off the beach?" I asked.

"Up to about forty pounds," Bob said.

We packed up the black Chevy and I climbed into the cab. Haines was driving and I was sandwiched between him and Bob. I felt secure between two grizzly, experienced fishermen, and excited about learning something new and maybe even catching a striper. Bob and Haines talked about people I didn't know, but I didn't ask a lot of questions. I just listened as they carried on. Haines would point out the occasional deer or woodchuck beside the road, seeming to have an extraordinarily keen awareness of his surroundings.

We rolled down through Fairfield to Southport, where I had spent many days fishing for blues with my friend Taylor, and we parked by the beach. It was pre-season, not quite Memorial Day, and a guard came up to check if we had a town sticker.

"Hello, ma'am, my name is Officer Haines"—he flashed his badge at her—"I was wondering if we could do a bit of fishing tonight."

"I suppose for a fellow officer," she laughed.

"I brought you a dozen clams," he said, fishing them out from behind the seat.

"Well," she said, "then I guess I'm going to have to let you fish, Joe."

She talked with us while we put on our gear. When we had finished we wished her good night.

Bob led the way down the large quarry rocks that supported the road from eroding during high seas. A creek came in to the right and thousands of small silver shiners and mummies darted back and forth. Haines pointed out a moss green crab in the clear water. Seabirds combed the low tide for bits of food. A tern dropped a mussel onto some rocks to crack its shell, and swooped down to pick up the meat.

"Once in a while I see ibis down here," said Haines, "but mostly it's egrets and gwaks."

"What's a gwak?" I asked.

"Black-crowned night heron. I call it a gwak 'cause that's

the sound it makes when it flies over." He paused, then continued walking, saying "gwak, gwak."

"What's that over there?" Haines asked me, pointing to a slim white bird.

"A snowy egret," I said.

"But do you know the difference between a snowy egret and a cattle egret?"

"I'm not sure."

"How about that old bird?" Bob interrupted, pointing at Haines.

"How about that?" Haines pointed back at Bob. "A dodo." We all laughed. I liked watching them kid around, but I wasn't quite sure where I fit in.

We walked on ahead, clusters of mussels crunching beneath our feet. Haines flexed his rod, preparing for fishing. I glanced to the right to see the row of mansions and their elegant sprawling lawns.

"If I had one of those," said Haines, "I'd be out fishing every night in my backyard."

The breeze was mild and began to die just as we moved from shore to water. There was a sea smell, and I could feel things all around me crackling with life. I wished the breeze would pick up just a bit to blow away the tiny bugs that swarmed around us.

"Everything has got to eat," said Haines as he lit a cigarette and waved it around, "but they don't have to eat me. This is the spot."

We were about waist deep in water. Bob walked off along the sand.

"See where I parked the car?" Haines asked. "Well, I park it there every time and there's a reason."

"What's that?" I asked, looking around.

"You see those pilings between us and the shore? Over there, about twenty feet high?"

"Yeah, I see them."

"When I line up the fourth piling with the truck, I know I'm in the right spot."

"The right spot?"

"See, we're about a hundred yards from the pilings. Out in front of us, facing Long Island, there's a sand bar. We're actually on top of it right now. But just beyond is a hole, which is sometimes exposed during an especially low tide. When the water's high and the tide's coming up, the big stripers move in. This is where you'll catch your first striper: off the beach. The sun's still got another half hour or so before it sets, and just in that twilight time I've got some of my biggest fish. I get some big ones in the dark, but I prefer dusk so I can see them hit the surface. Be sure to walk slow; the stripers could be right at your feet. You'll know if you've scared one in shallow water because you'll see a big boil." Haines had already rigged his rod and was ready to cast. He could see that I hadn't rigged my rod yet.

"What've you got there in your vest?" he asked me. I pulled out a plug about four inches long. It looked like a minnow with a black back and silver sides.

"That lure's gonna be a bit small," he said. "You'd better try this one." He handed me a plug about six inches long with a blue back and silver sides. It had some red near the head and a yellow eye with a black pupil. I tied it on my line and dropped it in the water to test it. It floated, and I picked it up off the surface and cast it.

I glanced over at Bob, who had already hooked a small blue-fish.

Haines could see that I wasn't sure how to retrieve the lure once I'd cast it. "You want to toss this out as far as you can, either straight out or to one side of you, even behind you. Part of the fun is, you never know where they'll be, they could be swimming through your legs."

"Has that ever happened to you?"

"Maybe, but I never knew it. Now, once the lure is out there you start to retrieve it, sometimes slow, sometimes fast." He turned the handle on the reel at varying speeds. "I prefer to slow down the retrieve, the darker it gets. Enough talking now. Get your line in the water. Can't catch a fish if your line isn't in the water. One more thing: Make sure to retrieve right up to the rod tip, because sometimes they'll follow it right up and smack it at the last minute."

Watching Haines as he fished, I noticed he jerked the rod as he retrieved the lure. I put about ten feet between us, casting continually and trying different retrieves. The ten feet became ten yards and then twenty. Not a wave crashed, and as I started to move again, a large fish boiled right in front of me, sending a wake that lapped against my waders. I turned to Haines to tell him what I'd seen, but he was too far away and I thought that if I yelled I might scare away another fish. Before I'd seen the boil, I hadn't believed that you could sneak up on a big fish. Suddenly I felt extraordinarily present in the water, my senses alive, as if everything before was just a dream. Light from the sun grew golden and gradually diminished, replaced by the glow of the city of Bridgeport. Lights from the mansions behind us began to emerge and just as I turned to admire them, I heard line screaming out with a hiss, and saw that Haines was fighting what looked like a good fish.

"James," Haines called; I ran to him, moving as fast as I could in my bulky waders. I nearly fell over myself several times in the sand. "He's still on," I heard Haines say as I approached. "I'll give you the rod and you can fight him."

"No, I don't want to take your fish," I said. But he handed me his spinning rod anyway. "Wow, that's a good fish. It's taking out so much line."

"Take it easy and keep your rod tip up. Not like that, UP! That's better. You'll land him if you do it right. This is a good fish, not a monster, but a good one. To land a monster, doing things right isn't enough. There are just too many things out of your control. A monster can bang his head on rocks or wrap you around a buoy or a piling. To land a monster, you have to be lucky."

To me, this fish *was* a monster. It took several runs, ripping line off the spool, thumped, and ran some more. When it was tired, it came to the surface, disturbed the evening calm.

"Don't drop the rod tip," Haines said again when I got him up close. "Just ease him by me and I'll grab him. This looks like a keeper, and I haven't had striped bass on my plate for quite a time." I was usually resentful when people tried to help me catch a fish, but somehow I didn't mind with Haines.

"What's a legal keeper?" I asked Haines.

"Thirty-six inches." I watched as Haines grabbed the fish and removed the hook from its mouth. Bob came over to admire it, too. "That'll look even better golden brown with some butter and bread crumbs," he said. I kept quiet. Though I didn't share their sentiments about the fish looking better on a platter, I respected them. It was a splendid fish, and I'd never seen Haines with such a smile. "Let's make sure it's legal," Haines said, and I pulled out a tape to measure it. It was thirty-nine inches. He fed a rope through the fish's mouth and out its gill, and tied it to a loop in his waders.

Haines had risked losing his fish to give me the chance to feel what he had many times before. Haines had hooked it, but I had landed my first striper.

By the time we decided to head back, there were only stars and a few lights from the mansions on shore. The tide was beginning to swallow us. We had been backstepping for a good hour as the water got deeper and the pilings that were once exposed became mostly submerged.

"If you walked straight back to the truck," said Haines, "the way we came out, you'd be underwater. We're walking back to shore on the sandbar and then walking the shore to the truck."

The smooth sand turned to a mixture of rock and sand, making the walking tricky. The big fish trailed behind Haines in the water. When we came to shore, he untied it from his waders and lifted it into the air. "Can I carry the fish for you?" I asked him. He handed it to me, and I slung it over my shoulder with a newfound pleasure: the triumph of the trophy.

———

Cooked blue crabs with butter

BLUE CRABS

I was standing in Haines's driveway when Bob's truck rolled in. A boy was sitting beside him. He looked lean and lanky next to Bob. "Oh, James," said Bob as soon as they had gotten out of the truck, "meet my nephew Carlo. He's visiting from the Carolinas."

I'd first heard Carlo mentioned while I was fishing one night off the beach with Haines and Gost. Haines told a story of Carlo hooking a huge striper, which dragged him across a sandbar. As the story goes, Carlo fought the fish for half an hour and then lost it. I didn't like the sound of it. A boy my age who might be able to fish as well as me?

"Nice to meet you," I said to Carlo. He looked at me, pale and vaguely uninterested. I can't say I felt very excited about the day either, and could barely push out a greeting.

"Hi."

"Well," said Bob, "I've got to get back to the machine

35

shop. Just give a call when you get back and I'll come and pick up Carlo. Be good," Bob said to Carlo. He pulled out his wallet and spoke quietly to him. I was just close enough to hear him say, "Don't let old Joe pay for your lunch," and saw as he handed him ten dollars. Bob got into his truck and drove away.

We were headed to Stratford, to see if we could catch some blue crabs. In the dead of summer, the trout streams were low and there weren't many bluefish running.

"Well," said Haines, "I suppose we should get the gear together. James, why don't you grab the minnow traps in the shed and the long-handled net." I rummaged around the shed, looking for the equipment, and brought it back to Haines. "That's not the right net," Haines said to me. "Let me show you which ones we use."

"Aren't these the ones we used last time we went?"

"No, I've got ones with even longer handles than those." We walked over to the shed. "Here, these are the ones." He took them and put them in the back of his pickup truck. "Let's hop in and go." Carlo jumped right into the cab, sitting in the seat next to Haines. I sat by the window and didn't say anything.

We were heading for the salt marshes, much of which had been paved over with blacktop. As soon as we crossed the town line, the temperature seemed to climb another ten degrees, heat radiating off the pavement. The blacktop on either side of the street held cars, industrial parks, and steel storage fields with enough I beams and coiled wire to circle the globe several times.

There were patches of marsh among the sections of blacktop, marked by clumps of reeds. Every once in a while a slight breeze, produced by an airplane taking off, would stroke them. Mostly, it was still and hot. Haines and Carlo chatted, and I stared out the window, wishing I had gone fishing instead.

Haines pulled the truck off at a general store. Carlo and I tagged behind him, following him to the meat section. I didn't have any idea what he was doing, and I'm sure Carlo didn't either. We watched silently as he selected a pack of chicken wings. We had to buy wings that weren't frozen, Haines explained—not that it really mattered in this heat. The store was air-conditioned and I bathed in the cool air before returning to the heat of the day.

Back in the truck, we headed for the marsh near the airport to catch the tide as it came in. I had a lot of memories from being with my father in the marshes: the sulfur smells, the fiddler crabs, the acres of tall reeds and grasses, the occasional sighting of a terrapin. My father taught astronomy in a nearby school, and during the summer he used to take groups of kids on nature field trips. I would always tag along, mostly for the ice cream we got on the way home. The trips had stopped several years ago, and suddenly I missed them.

We parked the big black Chevy and grabbed a minnow trap out of the back. Haines wanted to make sure we had the bait selection covered. We would have two options, the chicken wings and the minnows, called mummies, that we needed to catch. The trap was two identical pieces. Put together, it made a tube with cones of wire on each end pointing toward the center.

At the tip of each cone was a hole, into which, hopefully, minnows would swim.

Haines had chosen a favorite spot for trapping minnows, a little inlet from Long Island Sound. The inlet was just beyond the runway at Lordship, and planes kept taking off right in front of us, shimmering in the heat and booming overhead.

Haines baited the trap with chunks of old bread he pulled from his pocket and tossed it into the current caused by the turning tide. We tied the trap to the branch of a beach rose, *rosa rugosa,* as my father called it. The trap was in about two feet of water, and we watched the bread become saturated and sink to the bottom. We couldn't see any minnows near the trap, and thinking that watching it wouldn't much help, we walked a bit on the road that ran alongside the marsh. On the other side of the road was the sound, which was flat and perfectly still. We stood for a while, looking out silently. Through the haze you could see Long Island. I saw a distant boat, its sail hanging limp.

"Where do you get the crabs?" Carlo asked.

"Just down the road a bit," Haines said.

Haines turned from the sound and we trailed behind him as he walked back to the trap.

Haines pointed at it. "See those little black backs swimming all around the trap?" You could see the minnows, but not against the muddy bottom of the marsh; they were visible only as they passed over the white pieces of bread. From the number of mummies I saw, I figured we had a good load. Pulling the trap in, we saw about four dozen mummies, which Haines dumped in a bucket full of salt water. I sank my hand into the bucket thick with live minnows. The black mass was writhing, minnows slipping between my fingers.

A plane taking off from Lordship cut through the air above us. It was massive and booming and it briefly cast its shadow on me. A black-backed gull descended in a glide to see what scraps it could scavenge, knowing that the presence of humans often meant an easy meal. We got back in the truck, the bucket of fish stored safely on the floor next to my feet.

"What kind are we going for?" Carlo asked in his slight southern accent.

"Blue crabs," Haines said, "though you could probably catch crabs faster in the bathroom at Bridgeport Railroad Station." I had heard this crude joke before and supposed the repetition was for Carlo's benefit; Haines knew I didn't find it particularly funny. Haines parked, and Carlo and I helped him carry the mummies, buckets, and nets.

Haines instructed Carlo by a stand of reeds on the inland side of the bridge where we had parked the truck. Sticks, wrapped with a length of Dacron line, lay in a pile next to them. Salt was caked on from the last time they'd been used, and each line had to be tugged to get it off the stick. At the end of each line was a wire ring on which to place the bait.

"Take a mummy," Haines said, reaching into the bucket, "and string it onto the wire through the eyes. Then," Haines continued, "take about ten yards of line off the spool and toss it out into the water." Haines took the stick and pushed it into the mud near Carlo's feet. I was down the inlet a bit, setting up my own lines and watching impatiently, just able to make out the instructions. Although I'd been crabbing with Haines before, I wanted to hear what he was telling Carlo.

"There, your first line is set," Haines was saying. "Here's three more." He reached down and handed them to Carlo.

Haines was off to set one of his own lines, this time stringing a chicken wing on the wire.

Carlo had gotten the idea quickly and was setting his lines like a pro. I had set four lines myself and was waiting to see whether I had selected a good spot. Between us, we had a total of ten lines out, spread at equal intervals along the inlet. There was no overlap in territory; I had to set up to the right of Haines's lines, and Carlo to the left. There was no science to selecting a spot, no way to know exactly where the crabs would be. The set lines were all pulled taut from the current caused by the changing tide.

Haines had the first tug from a crab and offered Carlo the chance to pull it in. I came over to watch and saw the line wandering slowly to the right and then over to the left. I couldn't help but remember when Haines used to let *me* reel in what he'd caught.

"O.K.," said Haines to Carlo, "gently grab the line, and inch by inch start pulling him in. Can you feel him tugging?"

"He's on there all right," Carlo said.

"Now, take it slow and I'll get the net." Haines grabbed the long-handled net that he had set leaning against the reeds. It had a mouth of about eighteen inches across. He eased the net into the water and held it under the line, pressed against the bottom of the marsh approximately where the crab should appear. Carlo inched the line in, winding it around the stick.

"Just like that," said Haines. I took a step back so as not to interfere with Carlo's first blue crab.

"O.K.," said Haines. "I'm going to push the net out a bit more, then let you bring the crab over it." The crab walked directly into the net, its claws attached to the chicken wing. Haines lifted the net smoothly, bringing it out of the water and turning it over to try to dump the crab into the bucket, which sat empty between them. It was a good one, with tinges of deep indigo and two large claws; beautiful and fierce. The crab resisted, holding tenaciously to the pocked skin on the waterlogged chicken wing with one claw and the net with the other.

"Here, Carlo," said Haines, "hold the net so I can get him off. The proper way to hold a crab is either by both claws, if you can get them both at once, or by the rear of its abdomen, where neither claw can reach." Haines grabbed the crab by both claws and pulled until it let go. "There," he said, "and you'll see, it'll look even better cooked; fire-engine red on a plate or dipped in melted butter." When Haines walked away, I picked a reed and poked the end of it down into the bucket. The crab grabbed the reed and I pulled it up until it let go, falling back into the bucket. Haines turned and said sharply, "Don't play with your food."

His comment only reminded me that I hadn't caught any crabs yet.

After the excitement from the first crab died down and I had walked back to tend my lines, one of Carlo's lines started to move. "I think I got one," he yelled.

"Why don't you get the net," Haines called to me. I ran across the mud, which was slowly disappearing with the rising tide. I almost lost my shoe in the mud's moist suction. Carlo brought the crab in gingerly and I grabbed the net.

"Don't miss it," Carlo said.

I eased the net into the water as Haines had and when the crab was nearly to the net, I thrust out and missed it. The crab darted off with a speedy backstroke.

"Sorry," I said to Carlo.

"That's O.K."

Haines had the next crab on.

"Hey, Carlo, why don't you get the net and show James how it's done?" Haines said.

Naturally, Carlo netted it and added it to the bucket. I knelt down and played with the crabs a bit; I would have enjoyed watching them more if I had caught them myself. "Don't let James near the bucket or he'll tip it over and we'll lose dinner," Haines said. I couldn't really tell if he was joking. I stood up and went to check my lines. Everything seemed so competitive now, and I wasn't used to it.

Standing in my wet sneakers, I watched as across the marsh a snowy egret placed its yellow legs in the water without making a dimple in the surface. Maybe I'm not suited for this crabbing, I thought.

I pulled in one of my lines to check the bait. The soggy chicken wing was wrapped in what looked like a scarf of kelp.

The skin was covered with goose bumps and it was hard to imagine that at one time it had actually been part of a chicken. The skin was peeled away from the bone, and it looked like it had been nibbled on, probably by a less desirable spider crab. I removed the kelp and threw the whole thing back out into the water.

I pulled up my second line, which was baited with mummies. Two out of six of them were still alive, although they had been strung through the eyes. I tossed the line back, the splash of it on the water dwarfed by a yelp from Carlo, who had caught another one. Haines, naturally not trusting me with his dinner, grabbed the net while I relocated my third line between Haines's and Carlo's. A third crab made it into the bucket and Haines was so pleased he patted Carlo on the back. Crabbing takes no skill, I thought to myself. I'd like to see him with a fishing rod.

I decided I'd take a walk, and cut through the reeds in order not to pass by Carlo and Haines. I came out with six ticks on my legs, and I brushed them off one by one. The water in the sound on the other side of the road didn't look very clean, and there really wasn't much of a beach at all, but I was so hot I decided I'd take a swim. I peeled off my shirt and jumped in. While I was under water, an airplane from Lordship passed overhead, its engine reverberating like a motor boat. I floated for a while, enjoying the solitude, and then made my way back to shore. Putting on my shirt, I returned to my spot; the dried salt made my back itch under the fabric. I'm not sure they even noticed I was gone. It looked like there was a crab on one of my lines, the line farthest along the reeds, and I started toward it. In my haste to reach the line, my foot slipped on a rock and I fell in the mud. Since I hadn't announced that I'd had a bite and Haines and Carlo were still preoccupied with their own lines, no one saw me fall. I tried to hide the spreading dark spot on my shorts by pulling my T-shirt over it.

"I got one, I got one," I yelled, taking up the line in my hand.

Carlo grabbed the net and ran over. I could feel the crab, the vibrations telegraphed through the line.

"Ease the net in, Carlo," I said. "Please don't lose it." I knew if he had said the same thing to me, I would have been annoyed, but I couldn't help myself. Carlo slid the net into the water and pushed it out as far as he could while still being able to see its mouth. I led the crab to the mark. Carlo lifted, but not fast enough, and the crab escaped.

"Sorry," Carlo said, and I could tell he was.

"That's O.K. I guess we're even now."

" 'Bout time we should head out," Haines said. "We can stop on the way home and get some lunch." We loaded all the gear back in the truck and headed for a fast food place.

When we ordered, Carlo offered to pay with the ten dollars he had crumpled in his pocket, and Haines wouldn't let him. "Tell your uncle Bob to buy a membership to Weight Watchers," he laughed.

The air-conditioned room was a relief from the dry heat of the day, but my wet sneakers turned cold. I was too hungry to care. Eating our burgers and fries, Carlo asked if I wanted to fish the next day for bass on the lake in Bridgeport where his uncle lived. I hadn't been for bass in a while, and said sure, maybe I could show him the best spots for trolling. Haines just smiled.

Ten inch wild Brook Trout

CLOVER

"You ever seen a four-leaf clover?" Haines asked me. We were standing in the yard in front of his house.

"I've heard of them; they give you good luck, right? But they don't exist, do they?"

"They don't?" he said, and cracked a smile. "There's a bunch right here."

"I don't believe it."

"Well, why don't you look around a bit and then I'll show you one," Haines said.

I fell into the green lawn, crushing grass blades with my knees, and started to search. I crawled on all fours, looking intently in the scattered clover patches, which were a deeper green than the grass. Ten minutes must have passed, and I couldn't find one.

"I don't see any," I said to Haines, who had simply been walking around the lawn, picking up sticks and throwing them into the woods.

"There's one right in front of you," he said, "in the square foot around your left hand." I lifted up my left hand and looked.

"I still don't see it." Kneeling down, Haines plucked what he'd been looking at with his thumb and index finger.

"There," he said, laying it in my hand, "now do you believe me?"

"Can you find another?" I asked, testing him. He walked ten feet, knelt down, plucked another, and put it in my hand.

"Some areas have more than others," Haines said. "This patch seems to have quite a few." How he could distinguish a four-leaf clover from the others was astounding to me. He had a reputation for astonishing eyesight and the ability to spot wildlife from long distances. People who knew him said he could "track a mosquito over cotton."

"Well," he said, "my lunch break is over. Do you want to head out?" Haines had promised to take me to a native brook trout stream he had known about for some time. The Bridgeport Hydraulic Company had just sold a big parel of land up in Monroe, and the stream that ran through it was now legal to fish.

"Sure," I answered.

"All right, just follow me in your car. I'll walk you to the stream and then leave you there to explore." He got into his truck, I got into my car, and we drove off. It was warm and I wondered if any trout would be feeding in the middle of the day with the sun beating down on the water. The winding roads were tunnels through the canopy of leafy branches, the light burning holes in the cool shade. Haines drove north and I followed, up the familiar route to my cousins', and past Monroe High School. He turned off onto a road that I'd never been down.

On both sides white pines grew up straight and tall from a floor of dried needles. Haines stopped by a field and I pulled up behind him and turned off my engine.

"We've just got to walk a bit and we'll be there," Haines said. We walked up a hill and then cut into the woods. I was sweating, even though I was wearing shorts. Haines, who was dressed in long pants and long sleeves, must have been even hotter.

"You hear it?" Haines asked.

"Yeah, I think so."

"It's just up ahead." We walked up to the stream, which was tea colored, though clear enough to see to the bottom in most places.

"Boy," Haines said, "not quite as big as I remembered. Someone must be drawing water out of the stream. Even in the summer, this used to have more water in it. Let's see if there's still fish." He knelt down and turned over some leaves with his hand, grabbed a worm and put it on my hook. "Toss that out there," he said. Almost immediately, the line went tight and I pulled back; a beautiful little brook trout came tumbling out of the water and off the hook.

"That was a good fish," I said to Haines, "maybe eight inches."

"Not bad, but there's better ones in here. Let's keep going," he said.

The stream was flat for about a hundred feet where it crossed a field, dipping out of the woods and back in. On the other side of the field it transformed altogether, the gradient becoming steeper as it ran through a hemlock forest. Every rock in the stream was covered in a rich green moss, and hundreds of mosquitoes swarmed from every direction, landing on my arms and legs in droves. I frantically reached for the bug spray in my vest and drenched my skin with it, scattering the bugs.

"See, that's one reason to wear long pants and sleeves in the woods," Haines said, slapping a mosquito that had landed on the back of his neck.

We walked down a bit to the first large pool, about twenty feet across, and stopped.

"The water's kind of stained; tannic acid from the roots of oak and hemlock color it. Fish are usually a bit darker in hemlock forests like this. I've caught brookies that had black bellies." Pointing to a spot of sun in the stream he said, "Do you know the difference between a little minnow, like a blacknose dace, and a first-year trout?"

"Do baby trout have parr marks?" I asked, referring to the oval markings on juvenile trout.

"Yeah, they do, but even if you can't see the parr marks in the water, you can tell a fingerling trout from a minnow." He walked down and knelt by the stream. "You see those minnows that are darting around?" He pointed. "There must be a dozen of them."

"Yeah, I see them."

"Those are dace, but look at that little fish," Haines said, pointing again.

"Where, which one?"

"That one by the rock."

I looked in the direction he indicated, leaning over the brook until I could see my reflection, and finally saw the fish; it was tiny and the same color as the bottom of the stream.

"That's a little trout," he said.

"How can you tell?"

" 'Cause of the way it's holding in the current. See, it doesn't dart around in circles like the blacknose dace; it just holds perfectly still in the water with its tail just slightly cocked." The harder I looked at the fish, the more apparent it became that it was a trout. I could even see the tiny oval parr marks on its side.

"That fish must have been buried as an egg in the gravel last fall, and just emerged this spring. He might be three inches by winter. Cast down the bottom of this pool," Haines said, looking toward the end of the pool where a shallow run gave way to a deep hole. I cast and reeled in a bit, and a good brookie, maybe nine inches long, hit my line. "That's a better fish," Haines said as I grabbed the hook in my finger and turned it to let the fish go.

"Beautiful," I said.

"You did that right, the way you let that fish go without even touching it. If you're gonna keep it, then it's all right to handle it, but I've seen guys hold the fish out of the water a minute and then they think they're doing it a service by letting it go. Come back in a few minutes and that same fish will be floating downstream, belly up. Especially in summer, when the water's warmer, they're more vulnerable to disease. Even if it swims away it could get covered up with fungus and die."

Next came a defense of his way of fishing, keeping fish, as

opposed to my way of fishing, letting them go. "I'm all for catching and releasing the fish you catch," he said, "but I also like to catch a few to eat once in a while. These little brookies taste really good fried, but you won't see me coming back every day for more. I got maybe a dozen little brook-trout streams I keep to myself, and I'll fish a couple of them maybe once a year and take only four or five native trout, just enough for dinner for me and my wife, and then I won't come back to that stream till the next year. Not every person likes to go through the work of pushing through brush to fish these small streams, but one person alone can destroy a stream. I've seen a guy poaching in a trout stream on Hydraulic property catch dozens of trout when they were spawning and keep them all. That can't be very good for the stream. That's why it's good to keep them secret."

I was lucky that Haines had shared the location of the stream, and I wanted him to fish it with me.

"Do you want to take a cast?" I asked Haines.

"No, I can't be fishing, I'm on duty. I'll be heading back on the road in a minute." I cast into the hole and pulled another good brookie into the sunlight, about the size of the last one. It had swallowed the hook, and I had to handle it too much to let it go. I kept it; hung it on a tree branch near the water until I was ready to leave.

"Have you ever caught a brookie out of one of these little streams that was bigger than twelve inches?" I asked him.

"No, they don't seem to get much bigger than eleven or twelve; if you get one thirteen, that's a monster. Once, I got one seventeen. Seems as though the environment—the size of the stream and the amount of food—dictates their size. They don't grow any larger than the stream allows. But if you take that little brookie and feed it, like I've fed brookies in the stream by my house, or put it in a bigger pond, you could get it up to eighteen or twenty inches."

It occurred to me then, looking at Haines as he talked, that some have said that the same principle applies to people—that they cannot grow any larger than their environment allows. I planned to go off to college in the coming years, to have new experiences and to learn, but would I be any better off than Haines, who had lived in the same town his entire life and had no education past high school? He had learned a lot from a life of observation in the woods and would continue to learn the rest of his life; it was his curiosity that kept him searching for new experiences. Perhaps, then, there was enough within the square mile of where we stood to keep an inquisitive mind occupied for a lifetime.

"I've got to be going," Haines said, "but you don't have to go, James. Keep fishing downstream and let me know what you get." With that, he turned and walked up into the dark wood until he disappeared.

Kokanee salmon on seat cushion

THE DROWNED BOY

"You know, a boy died last night," a woman in a canvas jacket said to us as we walked down to the dock.

"A boy?"

"Yeah, they think it was the cook over at the Hotchkiss School—more like a young man, maybe. See those boats out on the other side? Well, I'm just here to tell fishermen not to go over there, 'cause they're looking for the body. They think he drowned."

"What happened?" I asked.

"One of the school canoes was out across the lake and they think he may have been drunk and fallen off. They think he may have got caught up in the weeds and couldn't swim."

"Well, ma'am, we'll do our best to stay away," Haines said. The woman turned and walked back up the boat ramp.

The day was breaking over the Litchfield County hills. It was a particularly cold morning for late August. We were in the town of Salisbury, in a village known as Lakeville, and were fishing

Lake Wononskopomuc, which Haines called Winiskopumuck. He wouldn't even try to say it right.

Bill Franklin, a buddy of Haines's, was pulling gear out of the truck while Haines and I went over to the boathouse to rent the boat for the day. I looked out of the boathouse door to see old Bill heaving the nine-horsepower Evinrude engine down to the dock. He was seventy-five years old.

"That'll be seven-fifty for a half day, thirteen for a full."

"Full day, please."

I handed Haines a twenty, offering to pay.

"James, don't be ridiculous. When you're rich someday, you can take me fishing in Alaska." I put the money back in my pocket.

As Haines was looking at the fishing lures for sale in the boathouse, I looked on the walls near the register. There were photos of bass after bass that must have been from five to eight pounds each.

"Did these come out of this lake?" I asked Haines.

"Probably, James," Haines said.

"Can we try for bass a bit?"

"Maybe as we shove off we can try some casts at the weed bed," Haines said as we walked out of the boathouse. "While I help old Bill put the engine on the boat and get it started, you grab the oars and some seat cushions for us over there." Haines gestured. "Just around the building where that railing is."

Around the corner of the building was another door, which I opened and walked through. In the corner, dozens of oars leaned against the walls, with metal rings clamped around their mid-sections and pegs that fit into the oarlocks on the boats. From the pile of boat cushions I grabbed three. They were bright orange, with the letters T.S. printed on them. Town of Salisbury, I thought.

"Good, James, you got the oars," Haines said when I had returned and put them in the boat that Bill had picked out.

"And the cushions."

"Well, we can get going if you're both ready. James, you sit in the bow, Bill can sit in the middle, and I'll sit in the back and work the motor."

I laid my two rods in the bow and made a little area for myself, enclosed by my tackle box and a net. The bottom of the old wooden boat had some water in it, more likely from rain than a leak, and there were two makeshift anchors: cinder blocks tied to rope.

"You ready, Bill?" asked Haines.

"Huh?"

"I said, ARE YOU READY?"

"Yeah."

Old Bill was, in contrast to his able physical condition, near deaf.

"See what I mean, James?" Haines said to me. "That's why I call him Huh."

"Huh?" said Bill

"Yeah," I said.

Haines maneuvered the boat out of the slip and navigated through a group of small sailboats. The lake was incredibly clear. I had never seen water like it—the bottom must have been fifteen feet below and still I could distinguish rocks from logs and could count the feathery tips of the milfoil weed that grew in tall strands from the bottom. Some of the weeds had grown so tall that they broke the surface and were starting to flower.

"Well, James, what are you waiting for? We're at the edge of the weed bed; get your rod ready. See the weed, it don't grow any deeper than about fifteen, twenty feet, so at this drop here there's an edge where the weed bed ends. The bass like to hang right on the edge of the bed."

I let Haines explain it to me, even though I knew all of it from reading fishing magazines. I could see that he took pleasure in it, so I let him continue. "There's probably a bunch of mud-suckers down there," he said. Trout and salmon were what Haines fished for mostly, but in the summer, when the streams got warm and the trout were less active, he returned to the sound to fish the beach for stripers and blues. He didn't have much respect for bass.

I put on a purple rubber worm and cast it to the weed bed. Letting it sink to the bottom, I began to lift it and drop it, lift it and drop it, until I felt a tug on the line.

"Hey, I got one," I said, and I saw old Bill lean over the boat a bit, causing it to rock. "It feels like a good one."

"Good," said Haines, "now that you got one, we can fish for salmon."

Pulling it to the surface, I grabbed the fish by the lower jaw and lifted it up to take the hook out. It was a two-pound bass.

"That's a nice fish," said Bill. "You suré you want to let that go?" I could see old Bill salivating as I eased the bass into the water and watched it swim away.

"You just let go Bill's dinner," Haines said to me. "Couldn't you see him eyeing that fish? He already had it smothered in butter, crackling in the pan."

"Huh?" said Bill. "Let me tune you in." He turned up the volume on his hearing aid.

"NICE BASS, I said," repeated Haines.

"Yeah, would have been nicer with butter in the pan," Bill said.

Lake Wononskopomuc is round, and at almost any spot you can see the lake in its entirety. We moved to a place off a sloping green lawn. A house was barely visible through the trees in the distance.

"Does this look like the spot?" said Haines to Bill.

"Yeah, does," said Bill.

Old Bill fished the lake a lot in the summer with an old friend and knew many of the places where the kokanee salmon hung out. We got out our spinning rods. I had one and Haines and Bill each had two.

"See, James, all's you do is tie a small hook, size eight or smaller, to the end of your line, and a lead shot about two feet up. Then take a piece of corn, put it on, and lower it to the bottom." Haines opened the bail on his fishing reel and let the line peel. "You can let it hit the bottom and then reel up a couple of turns. Never know exactly where they're gonna be, so I like to set one rod near the bottom and then one about halfway up from the bottom."

"How deep are we?"

"Oh, I don't know, fifty feet maybe?"

"How deep is this lake?"

"This is the deepest natural lake in Connecticut. The deepest spot is a hundred and four feet, but it's real unusual 'cause it's got these steep cones that come up from the bottom, like that island, but just off the island it drops off."

The sun had taken the morning chill away. I pulled off my flannel shirt and watched the goose bumps on my legs disappear. Rigging up my rod with a hook and a kernel of corn, I dropped it to the bottom.

"These kokanee got small mouths, that's why we use small hooks. Their mouths are real soft so they get off the hook sometimes pretty easy. If you hook one, James, be easy with him."

I looked over, opposite the boathouse where we'd launched from, to the Hotchkiss School boathouse. To the right of it was a small beach and off the beach were four boats that looked as though they were tied together. I could see one of the boats was a Boston whaler and two people in wet suits were sitting on the edge, their backs to me. As they plunged backward into the lake, I saw a third person come up, breaking the surface of the water.

"You think they're looking for that boy?" I asked Haines.

"Looks like it," he said.

Nothing moved on the water. The sun was high. I had the mixed feeling of hunger and dehydration that I get on a boat around lunchtime when I haven't eaten since 5:30 A.M. Haines and Bill continued to fish, but it had passed that certain acceptable period of time without a bite.

"Bill, you get any bites?" I heard Haines ask.

"Huh?"

"I said, you get any bites?"

"Nah."

There was a long silence, broken only by the shuffling of feet on the boat bottom. Bill jigged his rod slowly. Haines pulled off his cap and dunked it in the water.

"You know Nick Fingelli died?" Haines said.

"No. We were just up here last year with him, remember?" Bill replied.

"Yeah."

"What got him?"

"Cancer. Pretty bad. But he had some good years on the water, some real good years. Good man."

"Have you seen any dead people in the reservoirs?" I blurted out without really thinking. He jigged his rod a bit.

"I've found bodies on the sides of the road, just over stone walls. One guy was down in a well, dead, don't know if he fell in by mistake or what." "Found two people who'd hung themselves from trees. One was an older man. I climbed up the tree to cut the rope loose from the limb. Once, I found a kid who hung himself, 'bout your age." He shook his head. "But they did it to themselves," he said. We continued to fish, until a listless sleep overcame me, and I lay with my head against a seat cushion, my cheek warmed by the sun.

"James," Bill said, tapping me on the shoulder with a tinfoil-wrapped bundle.

"So," said Haines, "it's all too exciting for you. I thought you liked to fish."

"What's this, a sandwich?" I asked.

"Sufrite," Haines said.

"What's sufrite?"

"Hearts and livers fried with onions."

61

I unwrapped the sandwich to expose a beautiful Portuguese roll, and was then met with a pungent smell. I took a bite and didn't like the texture. I wanted to spit it out immediately.

"Hearts and livers of what?" I asked, trying to keep an open mind, given my hunger.

"Chicken."

"I don't quite like this," I said, trying to swallow the lump in my mouth.

"Don't eat it then," Haines said rather curtly.

I opened the sandwich over the water, letting the chunks of liver and heart tumble to the bottom. Now I was left with just a roll, warmed by the sun, that still carried the smell of onion. I ate half of it and then tossed the rest in the lake.

"Could I have a drink?" I asked in desperation.

"Yeah, you want a Coke?"

"Please."

I opened the Coke and guzzled half of it, stinging my sun-parched lips. I looked over toward the group of boats. Men were lifting a body out of the water. I could see that the dead boy was wearing jeans and a white T-shirt. We reeled in our lines and pulled up the anchor. Haines had decided that we should try trolling a little while for the kokanee. I think he wanted to have a closer look at the boy.

"Get out your lead-core line," he said.

The line we used for trolling is woven Dacron around a lead center. Every ten feet of line is a different color and sinks down about five feet when the boat is moving at trolling speed. After we had tied small silvery lures to our lines, we set our lines at different depths determined by the color.

We all watched the boats without speaking as they brought the body to shore. Two rod holders were clamped to the side of the boat, and I used one of them and set my rod in it so that I didn't have to hold it. The sun was hot on my face and I rested my head on the bow.

"Hey! James! You got one," Haines yelled, and I grabbed my rod to see if it was still there. He had only said it to wake me up.

We swept up and down the shoreline without any luck, and then Haines got a bite. "It's a good little salmon," he said, and far off behind the boat a beautiful silver fish leaped out of the water.

"They like to do that," Haines said. "Did you see that?" he added. Bill pulled out the net and stood up to see where the fish was.

"It's coming up, Bill." And just as Haines said that, the salmon leaped again and came off the hook.

"Oh, well, at least we found where some might be."

The path that we had taken to catch that salmon was along the shore by the Hotchkiss boathouse.

"Let's take a turn and try the same spot again," Haines said.

"How many colors did you get that one at?" I asked Haines.

"I was down to green. Six colors." Faithfully, I let my line down to six colors, thirty feet into the clear depths. As soon as the boat got up to speed my rod bent over in a lazy arc, resisting the pull of the water. A subtle tap vibrated up my pole and into the handle of my rod.

"I think I got a hit," I said.

"Well, just leave it down there, he might come back."

63

The hit came again, even more subtle the second time, and I pulled back. A little salmon leaped almost immediately out of the water, about sixty feet behind the boat.

"Did you see that?" I said to Bill.

"Huh?"

The fish looked to be only about eleven inches long, and given the weight of the lead line, I was surprised that I could even feel it. Old Bill stood up with the net and set it in the water. There was not a shake or trepidation in his large hands. I led the little salmon, now lying on its side and flashing silver, out from the cold deep water into the warm surface water and then into the net. Bill scooped it up. It flopped on the orange seat cushion, brilliant and sharp. And then he put it in the bucket.

"There's one for the pot," said Haines as he took the bailer, a cutoff Clorox bottle, and transferred some water from the lake into the bucket. The salmon, now feeble in the warm water, undulated as if it were swimming. I hadn't wanted to keep the salmon, but I liked the idea of contributing to Haines's meal.

"Let's make another pass through that spot," Haines said.

Every time, back and forth, we had a new view of the scene onshore. By now, they had brought the body of the boy to the dock. He was lying on his back, the sun in his unseeing eyes. The crowd of men who had helped find him moved to the other side of the dock, away from the body. We continued to troll back and forth for another hour, and the boy continued to lie there, unmoving, in the sun.

"Shouldn't they drape a sheet over him or something?" I said.

"Well, they probably don't want to touch him until the

coroner comes," Haines replied. "I don't think they are entirely sure how he died."

"They think he was drinking?"

"James, listen, you heard all that I heard, how do you expect me to know something that you don't?"

I wasn't hurt by Haines's obvious irritation. I knew that he was frustrated not to be able to answer my question, and the idea of the boy's death disturbed him, too, even though he would never admit it.

We pulled two more salmon to the boat and added them to the first one in the bucket. They circled in the warm water until their bright eyes glazed over and their silver sides became dull.

Another hour passed in the hot sun, and still the boy was on the dock, lying there in his T-shirt and jeans.

"Why can't they take him out of the sun?" I said again.

"James," said Haines, "is there a difference? Why not let him enjoy the sun? What's dead is dead and nothing can be done."

When we'd pulled the boat to the dock at the end of the day, the boy was still there, now surrounded by flashing red lights and a group of people, a barely visible small mound on a dock across the lake. If we hadn't seen him earlier, we wouldn't know what all the fuss was about.

Cows on Seeley Road

On Patrol

My father was ripping the old carpet out of the living room of our house. Beneath it were the old, wide-planked wood floors, which he would then strip and finish. I helped him carry the rolled-up carpet out to the garage and then listened as he called Rick, the man he had hired to haul the carpet to the dump, along with a few other things he'd been meaning to get rid of. Haines had mentioned that he wanted to take a few pieces of it to line the bottom of his aluminum boat, so that when you dropped something, the sound wouldn't scare the fish away.

I found Haines at home, on his lunch break.

"Hey, you want to pick up some pieces of the carpet before it gets taken to the dump?"

"Yeah, I'm just finishing up my sandwich and then I'll come by before I go back on duty. I'll leave in about five minutes. Bobber wanted a piece of it, too, for the workroom in his basement."

Rick drove up in his truck about ten minutes after I hung up with Haines, and my dad and I started to load the junk. Haines pulled into the driveway behind Rick's truck, walked up, and began to help load. It took three of us to move an old generator out of the back of the garage and into the truck. It was odd to see Haines and my father working together. I was what they had in common, and yet my relationship with each of them was so different.

"Should have told me you were giving this generator away, Lou," Haines said to my dad.

"Didn't think you'd have wanted it."

"Why don't you take it now?" I asked Haines. "It's going to the dump."

"No, James, your father already gave it to this guy," he said pointing to Rick.

Haines pulled out his knife and rolled out a piece of the carpet to cut.

"What are you going to use that old carpet for, Joe?" my dad asked.

"Well, my friend Bob Gost wants to put a piece on the floor of his workroom, and I wanted a chunk to put in the bottom of my aluminum boat to reduce sound. Nothing goes to waste, Louey. I've been scrimping all my life, it's just the way I am. I sold a load of wood to a guy the other day and he must have looked at my old clothes and beat-up truck and felt sorry for me, 'cause he gave me a hundred-dollar bonus."

"That's just what James does," my dad said. "He wears his shoes until his toes are coming out of them and his socks have holes and he won't buy new ones. It's like he wears his stuff until

I feel sorry for him and you know what? It works, don't ask me why. He must have learned that from you, Joe," my dad said.

I looked down at my shoes and at my toes which were coming out of them. Without being entirely conscious of it, I realized I had started to dress a bit like Haines. I wondered when my dad had noticed.

Haines rolled up his piece of carpet and put it in the back of his truck.

When we were finished, Rick secured the tailgate and my dad paid him.

"Listen," Haines said, "I'm on duty soon, and I'm going to run down the street here for a quick look at the reservoir. There's been a report of people swimming down there. You want to come along?"

This was an irresistible opportunity. I would get to patrol the area I frequented the most, with the very man who had caught me trespassing so many months before. I figured I knew the woods that surrounded the reservoir as well as he did, maybe even better.

We drove to the end of my street and Haines got out of the truck to unlock the metal gate that I always jumped over to access the dirt road that led to the reservoir. He swung it open wide, and we drove through. I kept glancing out of the truck, scanning the woods, expecting to see *myself* running between the trees. We drove down behind Kaechele's property, and onto Bridgeport Hydraulic Company land. A yellow sign that I had passed many times was prominently displayed on an old sugar maple by the road: PUBLIC WATER SUPPLY. NO TRESPASSING, HUNTING, TRAPPING, OR FISHING. SAFEGUARD YOUR WATER

SUPPLY. I'd noticed that the new signs had replaced *trapping* with *swimming*, because no one trapped anymore.

"Do you put up those signs?" I asked Haines.

"Yup," he said tersely, obviously not wanting to discuss it further. He knew I never paid attention to them.

We drove down the hill and Haines shifted into four-wheel drive to get over a log that partially blocked the road. We stopped as the road sloped down toward the reservoir, and got out of the truck.

It had been a dry summer and the Easton Reservoir was low. Large expanses once covered with water were exposed. The shore was mostly loose rocks, left from the action of the waves which eroded the soil.

"This is a good spot to look for arrowheads," Haines said as we walked over a flat area usually covered by water. He had his eyes fixed on the ground; I followed his lead but didn't see anything unusual.

"Here," he said, "look at this." He bent down and picked up something, and then placed a small chip of stone in my palm.

"See this? It's flint. There's no natural flint around here. The Indians traded quartz for flint with natives that lived in what's now New York State."

"This was broken off while an Indian was making an arrowhead?" I asked, turning the gray chip in my hand.

"Yup," he said. I followed Haines back to the truck and we continued on, driving on the fire trails. I remembered seeing logging trucks stacked with timber come up through the woods several years ago. They'd stopped logging but had left large cleared areas in the woods. These expanses were open to the sun and had given way to thousands of black birch saplings and great patches of what I'd always called wild raspberries, but which Haines informed me were actually called wineberries. Clumps of red berries caught Haines's eye and we stopped. I didn't tell him I'd been in this exact spot, eating berries, just a week before. I wasn't sure if he would mind. They were a sharp scarlet color, very sticky and very sweet. After I'd eaten about three dozen, I noticed that they were covered with tiny green bugs, and that I must have swallowed a thousand of them. I didn't mention the bugs to Haines; he'd probably eaten as many as I had. We got back in the truck and moved on.

We came to the crest of a hill that I had walked over many times, under a grove of towering white pines. I had once seen a great horned owl and one of its young being chased by a flock of crows through the tops of the trees.

"See these pines?" Haines said. "These were planted many years ago. When I was a kid, there used to be a park here, with picnic benches. Up through the woods there's an old stone place to build a fire and grill hot dogs." I knew the crumbling structure he was talking about and had always wondered what it was, but I kept silent.

The road turned to the left and we stopped when Haines spotted a bluebird. We watched a small flock of six birds, two of them brilliant blue males, as they flew off into the woods. The fire trail wound back down to the reservoir and we drove by a long row of perhaps twenty large sugar maples.

"You know why there's a perfect row of sugar maples in the middle of the woods?" he asked me. I remember my dad asking me the same question as we stood in front of the very same row of trees this past winter, when all the leaves had fallen and all that was left was branches and sky.

"There was a house there, right?" I said. "And the people who lived there planted them."

"Yup. If you walk back behind them you'll see the old foundation." I, of course, already knew that. I'd spent whole afternoons looking in the cracks of the basements for shards of glass and pots, old coins, bottles, and other signs of the past. Trees grew through kitchens, vines wrapped themselves about the cracked hearths. Once in a while, I'd try to imagine a native Indian chasing a deer or a farmer building a stone wall. There was so much history in the woods. Stone walls ran in every direction and oftentimes you could judge the temperament of the farmer simply by the way he built his wall. Some were hurried piles, and others were works of art, a combination of serious skill and labor. Many of the walls had been smashed by fallen trees. Eventually, I supposed, they would all come down.

As Haines drove, I wondered why he had taken me along. It wasn't just to teach me things. I imagined that it got lonely—day after day riding along the same tracks in the woods, looking for poachers. Had he lost some enthusiasm that he hoped I could help him recapture?

Haines stopped the truck by a spot that I called Cove 5. I had named all the major coves by number, from the dam up to a patrolman's white house whose lawn bordered the reservoir at its north end. There were ten coves, and Cove 5 was definitely a favorite. It was shallow toward the inside and then dropped off in the middle. There was a huge boulder I liked to stand on to catch the large smallmouth bass that lived beneath it. Now, with the low water conditions, much of the inner cove lay exposed. Haines pointed to a half dozen mergansers that were standing on the shore. I saw them briefly, sturdy on their brilliant orange legs, before they took off across the sky. I suddenly missed fishing the reservoir. Now that I was legal, at least for the most part, it had been months since I'd fished it. I had always felt that the reservoir was mine, I was its exclusive fisherman, and now I could only look. But there was something about seeing it with Haines, having him point out things I already knew, and some I didn't, that gave me a different kind of pleasure.

"See that?" Haines said, pointing on the ground as we headed back to the truck. "Turkeys turned over the leaves there, looking for grubs and acorns." I remembered a time when I had been fishing near a downed tree, just off the shore, and I had heard a loud crackling sound farther up the hill, like a person walking. My heart racing, I had quickly hidden my fishing rod under the bank and walked slowly up the hill. Peering over a stone wall, I saw about two dozen wild turkeys, scratching in the leaves.

Haines saw a small pickerel frog and grabbed it.

"Let's feed the bass," he said. We walked out on a stone wall that sloped down into the water, and Haines tossed the frog about fifteen feet in front of us. It kicked on the surface and a small sunfish came up to nip at its toe. Then, out of the dark, a bass came up and ate the frog with a quick splash. I picked up a small stone off the wall and threw it.

"Bet I can throw a rock farther than you," Haines said, a young boy's smile on his face. I looked at him, a white-haired man near sixty. How could he throw a rock farther than me? We each went about selecting the right stone. I chose a round one that fit comfortably in my hand, and he picked one that was oval and flat.

"You throw first," he said. I threw my stone from a standstill off the wall, and it flew a decent distance, I thought. Then Haines threw his stone and it went half again beyond mine.

"How did you do that?"

"Flat stones fly farther in the right wind," he said. I figured one day soon I'd come out and practice.

And again we drove, north up the Easton Reservoir, past Cove 9, where I'd caught one of my biggest bass, past the spot where I once saw two guys swimming across the reservoir, and then up to the right where we would exit into the town of Trumbull. As Haines talked, I kept an eye out all along for poachers, wondering what would happen if we saw one. Haines lit a cigarette.

"We're going to end up out Seeley Road," Haines said, "where I grew up." But before we exited the property, Haines spotted a patch of steak mushrooms, as he called them, and some wild leeks. He got out of the truck to dig up the leeks and cut the mushrooms with his pocketknife. "Fry the mushrooms in a little olive oil till they're tender," he said as he handed them to me.

We drove up out of the Hydraulic property, onto a street lined with modest houses.

"When I was a kid, our house was one of the only ones on the street. That's it there," he said, pointing toward a single-level brown house. "Mostly there was just woods. I used to hunt and trap this whole area. Right there"—he pointed to a field where some cows lazily grazed—"in the swamp behind the field, is where I used to get a lot of my muskrats."

If he had trapped and hunted here, then our territories certainly must have overlapped. Haines grew up in the same forest as I did; some of the larger trees had witnessed the passing of us both. How could he really keep me out of these woods when he knew that I loved them as much as he had?

Haines was a patrolman for sure, but he was as much a boy in the woods as I was. I imagined a young Haines with a gun racing through the trees after squirrels and setting traps in the swamp for muskrats. The woods from his time had receded to the boundaries of the reservoir property, large farms and miles between houses only memories.

Haines and me on Selkirk Shores

SALMON RIVER

I tossed in my hotel bed. Haines was in the bed next to mine, snoring. He had left the TV on and I figured it must help him fall asleep, so I hadn't said anything. I couldn't sleep with the TV on, though, and now that he was snoring I felt it was all right to turn it off.

The heat in the room had been cranked up high, and when I got up my head was heavy and I felt dizzy. Oh, God, I thought, please don't let me be sick. I had taken off from school to go on this fishing trip and now I was going to be sick. I pushed the knob on the television and got back under the sweat-soaked sheets. The blanket had been tucked in so tightly at my feet that I couldn't pull up enough of it to cover the rest of my body. Curling up, I tried to sleep but only drifted in and out for what seemed like hours. I thought about our ride up to Pulaski, New York, the day before.

• • •

We had been on the Taconic Parkway, heading north. I was sitting in the back of the big black van that belonged to Don Halsted. He had lent it to us for the trip and was coming up to meet us later that evening. I reclined in the comfortable seats in the rear of the van, while Haines was at the wheel and Brian Favreau sat next to him. Beside me were five large bags of apples that Haines had brought from the orchard. Brian had a big wad of chewing tobacco in his jaw and when I offered him an apple he declined. Haines was smoking a cigarette, so I didn't bother to ask him. One bag was filled with Macouns, one bag Red Delicious, Yellow Delicious, McIntosh, and King David. Within an hour I'd tried them all, more out of curiosity than hunger.

We were at the head of a caravan of vehicles, all brought together by Haines. The enthusiasm ran high among the men. They were out of work for a week and away from their wives, hoping to take advantage of the salmon that were running in the tributaries of Lake Ontario. I was not escaping a job or spouse. I was simply there, feeling the October air through the window and thinking that I'd like to see a king salmon. I had never seen one alive before.

"James, wake up!" Haines yelled to the back of the van, even though I was awake. "See the creek under this bridge? All the salmon that come up the Salmon River come to this creek, and this creek leads to a hatchery."

"How do the salmon know that the creek leads to a hatchery? Why would a salmon want to go there anyway?"

"The way I've been told is that the salmon are imprinted on a smell when they are just an inch long. The hatchery releases that smell down this creek to the Salmon River and into Lake Ontario. Once the salmon find their way to the hatchery, the biologists squeeze out their eggs and milt and raise the little salmon until they are big enough to put in the lake."

"Seems kind of rotten that people have got to do it for them. Spawn, I mean."

"Well, James, it makes for a good fishery. After four years in the lake they are ready to come up the rivers to spawn. They can be bigger than forty-five pounds. The hatchery can raise more salmon than the river could produce itself."

I looked off the bridge into the water and saw a large salmon finning in the current. It must have been four feet long.

"That's a king salmon," Haines said.

And with one push of its tail that seemed to displace all the water in the creek, it spanned five pools and was out of sight.

"Can we chase it?"

"No," said Haines, "no fishing here."

"James! Wake up! I've been shaking you for a good five minutes." I opened my eyes to see Haines standing over me.

"What time is it?"

"Five-thirty," said Haines putting on his cap. "Man, I've

got this shooting pain in my tooth. It was bothering me all night."

Yeah, didn't hinder your snoring, I thought to myself. I didn't tell him that I was feeling feverish. I wanted to see how long I could survive without saying anything, refusing to believe that my trip could be spoiled by getting sick.

"Let's head off to the diner; we're supposed to meet everyone there."

We walked out of the room into the parking lot. The streetlights reflected on the hoods of parked cars. It was cold and I felt chilled to the bone. My mouth was dry and my head was spinning. We walked next door to the diner and settled into a booth.

"I'll have a fried egg on a hard roll," said Haines.

"The same," I said.

"How's the fishing been?" Haines asked the waitress as she started walking away.

"From what I hear, there aren't many fish in the river," she broadcasted as she grabbed the coffeepot and turned around to pour Haines a cup. My spirits sank even lower after the poor report. "Where you guys from?"

"Connecticut."

"Well, I hope it was worth the trip."

What a strange place, I thought, where the waitresses are in tune with the salmon migration. Every person in the diner was a fisherman. You could tell by their apparel. BOB'S SPORTING GOODS hats. KISS MY BASS T-shirts. Vests filled with tackle. If there weren't any salmon in the river, there would be a lot of unhappy fishermen.

As it stands today, Pulaski is the Las Vegas of the fishing world. Everyone comes to take their chances with the fish, but no one really knows when they will come up the river. The entire Salmon River fishery is fabricated. The salmon are originally Pacific Ocean fish, the brown trout were introduced from Europe, and the steelheads and rainbows are also coastal Pacific fish. Before they put these popular game fish in the Salmon River, no one drove hundreds of miles to fish it, because no one had ever heard of the little town through which it ran. Pulaski, once a farming town, now had a large strip of fishing-tackle stores and guide services. Farmers traded their hoes for fishing rods and guided visitors out on the river.

"A lot of fishermen here," I said to Haines.

"Yup." He bit into his egg sandwich that oozed yolk as he lifted it.

"Where are we going to fish today?" I asked Haines.

"Not quite sure yet."

"You think there'll be fish in the river?"

"You know as well as I do, James, I haven't been down there yet to see. But there are very few times when there are no fish to be had at all. The water is just a bit low, but if we got some rain tonight, the fish might all come up out of the lake at once and we would have our hands full tomorrow. What do you say, should we give it a try?"

"Sure."

I knew then that Haines was upset by the waitress's report too, although he hadn't said anything. He had organized the trip and didn't want everyone to be disappointed. Especially me.

Brian came with us down to the river. We didn't have to

drive very far, and when we came to a lot we parked next to some thirty other cars. Our gear was packed in the back of the van. Haines pulled out my waders and handed them to me. I put on one leg and then felt as if I might collapse, so I sat on the van's back bumper and put my head in my hands to stop it from spinning.

"You all right, James?" Brian asked.

"Just a bit sick, I think, but I'm trying not to let it get to me," I said.

"Here, you can use my shoulder to balance while you put on your waders."

The banks were lined on the opposite side with deep green hemlocks, and a crisp breeze blew through their branches. As I walked, I focused mostly on the ground, because I felt delirious, near stumbling. The more I breathed and the more space I had, the better I felt. The mad rushing of the river opened up into a placid pool.

"This has always been a good spot," Haines said, pointing now to the far end of the pool. "See that pair of salmon out there?"

"No," I said. Forced to look up, I noticed Brian was no longer around. And then, right where Haines pointed, there was an eruption as the pair of fish exposed their backs and thundered through the riffles.

"There's a few in here," Haines said, "just not as many as there usually are. Let's rig up our lines and see if we can get one. Give me your rod a moment and I'll show you how to set it up. You take the end of the line and tie it to this swivel here. Then cut the line up about three feet and tie the line from the reel on the other end of the swivel. What you've got is a swivel now tied to the line and three feet of line beyond it. Make sure to leave the excess line from the knot below the swivel, 'cause that's where we're going to attach the weight. Put on as much weight as you need to bounce the bottom of the river. We'll put a heavy steel hook and a single salmon egg on the end of the line."

"Why would a salmon eat a salmon egg?"

"I'm not sure if they always do. The line sometimes catches them in their mouth as it is drifting by and they get hooked. That's called lifting. I have seen salmon chase an egg though, as hard as that may be to believe. Now that it's all set up, you cast upstream and across, and let it drift with the current, so that the weights bounce the bottom."

"Like this?"

"Yeah, but lift up the tip of your rod a bit so you can see the tip of it tick as the weight bounces."

I bounced and bounced in the most tantalizing holes for salmon and nothing came. After a while, I went to sit in the grass to hold my head again. I laid my rod down in a plume of grass, and sitting in the water, I rested my head on the bank. The sky appeared before me, brilliant and blue and the clouds formed swimming salmon. Just then, a sound broke the stillness. Haines had a salmon on.

"Oh, don't lose it," I said as I walked over. I wanted at least to see a salmon up close, even if I couldn't catch one.

"Come over here, James, and take the rod."

"No, I couldn't. It's your fish."

"James, in my years I have caught many salmon. This one is yours."

I took the rod and struggled with the large fish, trying to get a good foothold on the slippery bottom.

"Keep the rod tip high. Fight him with the rod tip." And as I lifted the tip of the rod, I mapped the course of the huge fish's run upstream, which ended with a leap. The salmon broke through the surface of the water beyond where Haines was standing. Suspended laterally in the air, it dwarfed Haines's head.

"My God, that *is* a huge fish," I said. The line suddenly went slack.

"Is he gone?"

"Looks like it."

My sickness had momentarily disappeared while that fish was on but I felt it rushing back.

"They are something, those salmon," said Haines. " 'Bout time we got on to another spot. As soon as we find Brian, we can head out."

We drove toward Lake Ontario, hoping that there were more salmon near the mouth of the river. Haines pulled the van into the driveway of a small white farmhouse and grabbed a plastic bag out of a cooler in the back of the van.

"Hold on a second," he said to Brian and me.

We sat in the van, waiting for Haines. I watched him as he approached the stoop. As he walked, the door of the house opened and then the screen door was pushed wide. Framed neatly in the vestibule was an old lady in a patterned dress, with slippers on her feet. Haines lifted his hand to take both of hers, and after some talk and an exchange of smiles he handed her the bag.

"What did you give her?" I asked Haines as he adjusted himself in the driver's seat once more.

"A pair of lobsters."

"What for?"

"Every year we come up and park on her property to access the river, and every year I bring her something to show my appreciation. You can't accept a favor without giving something in return. Up here in New York State they don't have fresh seafood, so I bring her either a couple dozen clams or live lobsters. I used to give them to her husband but he passed on."

We drove through a field of corn, which had wilted since summer. A couple of pieces of corn still clung to the few upright stalks. Parking at the edge of the field, we grabbed our equipment and descended a large hill down to the Salmon River. I stood in the river casting until my legs were too cold inside my rubber waders. When my feet were numb, I would retreat to the edge of the stream and soak in the last moments of the sun, which was disappearing behind the clouds. My hands smelled of anise, which is what the eggs we used for fishing were scented with.

A light drizzle had begun to fall and mingled with the cold sweat of my fever. We decided to move on, our next destination the mouth of Grindstone Creek at Selkirk Shores, Lake Ontario. Although the weather made me feel even worse, Haines had mentioned that a good rain could trigger a salmon run up the river. The van had the windshield wipers going to keep the drizzle off, but somehow it clung to the glass. My first view of Lake Ontario was through the windshield, a mixture of gentle waves, miles of water, and raindrops.

"I have hardly ever seen the lake this calm," Haines said. Finally, I thought to myself, a positive word on the day's conditions. We put on our waders. Haines and Brian both had long rods for casting far distances into the lake. I had a shorter one made of fiberglass and an old reel with relatively light line.

"This is just like striped-bass fishing off the beach at home," I said as we walked over some sand down to the shore. The sand beneath our feet turned to rocks, smoothed by time. To our left was the mouth of Grindstone Creek, and as its name suggested, between the action of the river coming in and the waves rolling into shore, there was a sound of rocks gently polishing each other. Standing at the edge of the lake, a light wave occasionally lapping our feet, I saw an immense fish jump completely out of the water about a half mile offshore.

"Did you see that?" I asked Haines.

"See what?"

"That fish jump clear out of the water. It was unbelievable. There's another."

"Must be a salmon," Haines said, "unless it's a steelhead. Too far to tell. I've never seen that before."

There was no one around, and it felt as if we had found another world.

"You know," Haines said as we waded out into the lake, "you can never see it all; every day I see something new. That's why I can't stand it when someone's going on about all they know, that the salmon come in on such and such a day, and we catch them on this day every year. I've been coming up here twenty years and every year it's different. Like now, I don't think I've ever seen the lake this calm."

I was feeling a bit better, hopeful that I might actually catch a fish. Feeding the line through the guides on the rod, I put on a Finnish minnow imitation called a rapala. I cast it out, and as soon as it hit the water an enormous swirl engulfed it. The line zipped off the reel and I felt the weight of a good fish. And just as soon as it had been there, it was gone.

"Holy shit! That was a big fish!" I yelled and repeated it several times more to myself.

"What was it?" asked Brian.

"I don't know, but it was big."

"What were you using?"

"Three-inch rapala silver-sided black back."

"Boy, oh, boy," Haines said to Brian. "I never heard James so worked up and swearing. You could probably hear him hollering back in Connecticut."

Not long after, I hooked a second fish, and realizing that I was unprepared to combat it with my light tackle, I accepted the fact that I would probably lose it. This fish was not as big as the first, but by my standards it was huge. It was bumping its head in the sand, just like a striper does, to get loose from the hook. When I had it close, Brian grabbed the net and deftly landed it. The fish was a seven-pound lake trout. It had a background of blue-black and gray with white- and cream-colored spots on top. The mouth of the fish was relatively large compared to other trout I'd seen. It was my first laker.

"My God, it's beautiful," I said.

"Yeah, but it's a laker. They're not very respected as a game fish," said Brian, releasing a stream of black spit from his mouth.

"Why not?"

" 'Cause they don't fight as good as salmon, steelhead or rainbows."

"Well, I think it's a fine fish," and holding it by the tail, I rocked it gently in the cold water and then let it go.

"Nice fish," yelled Haines, as he had continued to cast.

"Thanks."

Evening filtered into the sky. I stopped casting to warm up onshore and to look around me. There was a large cement pier on the right with one lone fisherman at the end. He was the only other person in sight. The lake was vast, bigger than any lake I'd ever seen, and even bigger than Long Island Sound. Brian was suddenly shouting, disrupting the calm.

"Fish on." Brian's rod was bent in an arc, and he was straining as he fought. "It's a good fish," he said as I came closer. "Get the net." I turned in my path, to go get the net.

"Wow!" I said as I saw the fish jump, "looks like a rainbow trout." I saw its back as it raced by us.

"I've never seen a trout that big," I said. "It must be seven inches thick in the back."

"O.K., James, now I don't want to lose this fish, so you've got to listen to me when you go to net it. He's starting to tire, and as I bring him close you ease the net into the water. Don't plunge it, just ease it and I'll bring him to you." I eased into the water. I was probably more excited than Brian. He led the fish by me, and as I pushed it toward him, the trout sped around and almost through my legs. It bumped the rim of the net as I lifted it up, empty. A feverish chill ran through me, and I wiped my forehead, suddenly feeling a little sick again.

"He's still on, James, and you'll have another chance. Just keep the net there and I'll ease him in." I admired Brian's calmness.

"God, that is a huge fish," I said as I lifted up the net, landing it. When we got to shore Brian shook my hand. Haines came over to see the fish as I lifted it by its jaw and then weighed it on a spring scale.

"Twelve pounds, Brian! It's twelve pounds."

We were all excited when we left Selkirk Shores and felt that we had somehow beaten the crowds by discovering a lesser known and fantastic fishery. It was now nearly dark.

Back at the Redwood Motel, we washed up for dinner and then walked across the street to the Ponderosa Restaurant to meet the rest of our party. It was an inexpensive, all-you-can-eat type of place. After a long day of fishing I think anything would have tasted good.

We seated ourselves at a group of tables within talking distance of each other and Halsted stood and spoke.

"I think we all know the man who brought us all together here. In case you don't, he's the man with less white hair than me over there in the corner. You've all heard it, but I'm going to tell you anyway, the story of how I came to know old Joe.

"I was fishing at Saugatuck Reservoir and had my two lines out fishing for trout. In a short time I had a fish on, a respectable fourteen-inch rainbow. I heard a voice from behind me where moments ago there was no one. The voice said, 'Where I go we use trout that size for bait,' and turning around I see a man dressed in a green uniform who apparently meant business. As it turns out, this was my first meeting with Injun Joe, and the things I learned from him over the years I can't begin to enumerate. And speaking for myself, a man who had experienced a great deal in the outdoors and was already advanced in years, that means a lot."

Haines smiled.

"Funny," Bob Gost said, "I never learned anything from Joe." And we all laughed. The days spent separately were recapped for the group. Haines told everyone about the big fish that I lost.

"You should have heard James swearing and hollering when that big fish broke his line down at Selkirk Shores. Probably could've heard him all the way down in Connecticut."

We returned to our rooms after dinner and Haines flipped on the TV.

"Well, James, how do you like it up here?"

"Not bad, I just wish there were a few more fish around."

"Not much we can do about that," he said, sounding a bit hurt.

"Oh, I know. I didn't mean it that way."

"Tomorrow morning early you can get in a bit more fishing before you go back home to school. I think the Greenbergs are going back about noon."

When I lay down, my head began to spin again and I pulled my cover off because I was sweating. The television was on, but Haines had compromised by turning off the sound.

"Does the TV bother you, James?"

"No, it's all right," I said. At least he asked.

After several minutes Haines resumed the snoring that had kept me up the night before. But somehow now, I was comfortable with the snores that resonated through the room, sounding like a repeated attempt to breathe water. The droning lulled me into a deep, aquatic sleep.

Small brookie caught at Wolf Pit

WOLF PIT

My friend Josh had a growing fascination with raising trout and had begun to inquire locally about trout farms. He combed the yellow pages for a hatchery and found a small private trout seller in Bethel, on Route 58. We called ahead and arranged with the man who owned the hatchery to go up and see it.

There was no number on the mailbox but from the road we could see a circular cement tank. We parked near it and looked in. The tank held several hundred gallons of water that were circulated by a pump. Josh and I were admiring the large rainbow trout swimming in it when a tall man with a beard appeared. "Are you the boys who called?" he asked.

"Yeah," Josh said.

"Well," he said, not even introducing himself, "it's a small operation, but that's where I hatch them"—he pointed to a barn—"and that's where I put them when I've got them up to about two inches," he added, looking into the cement tank.

Inside, the small red barn was cool and musty. Trays for the fertilized eggs were stacked in the corner. "I hatch only rainbow trout. They spawn in the spring, ripe at about early April. I take a female first and push down the belly from the head back to get the eggs to come out." He performed the procedure in the air with his hands, since he had no fish to demonstrate with. "With the male, you do the same thing, take him and gently push from the head down on the belly and the milt, or sperm, comes out. All in the same bowl, 'cause next thing you do is mix it all up and then put them on these screens. You keep them on the trays in the dark for a couple months. It has to be in the dark, and with enough time you got little fish. The first thing you'll recognize in the egg are the eyes; just a pair of little black dots."

A barn swallow that seemed to have missed its cue to head south swooped by the entrance to the barn as I looked out. I saw the blue October sky and a few leaves falling. A dry breeze filled the barn and I wondered what made it feel so damp until the man knelt down to show us his water source. Lifting up a floorboard, he revealed what was nothing less than a secret world. There was water down there, bubbling up under the barn! "I built the barn over this spring," the man said. "This is my water source for the operation. It runs through the eggs when they are developing and keeps the tank full. It works out pretty well, but I probably won't be doing it much longer. Selling the trout to markets and fishing clubs brings in a bit of extra money, but I don't need the bother anymore.

"Let me show you something else," he said, and led us out

of the barn. Just off the entrance, about twelve yards, was a tiny stream, which I had not even noticed before, though we had just walked past it. It was overgrown with grass and trees, but peering through the wall of leaves, I saw the little brook. "Now, you won't believe me, but there are trout in here. Not those introduced rainbows, but native brook trout that have been here since the beginning."

"The beginning?" Josh asked.

"Of time," he said, "and this spring contributes to the beginning of Wolf Pit Brook. Down a bit where the stream gets bigger," he said, pointing north, "there's trout that are a bit bigger, all native fish."

"All wild?" I asked him.

"You bet, all wild fish. I haven't fished down there," he said. "I've caught only a few tiny ones here in my yard. But my neighbor told me he used to go down there and get some good ones. But it's been ten years or so since arthritis got him so bad he stopped fishing."

The man pointed across Route 58 and said, "The brook runs through the hollow over this hill, down through that state park over there. Listen, I've got to be heading out, but you boys should give it a try." We thanked him and got in the car.

"Let's go fish the stream," Josh said immediately. "Did you bring your rod?"

"Yeah, but I don't really believe the guy," I said.

"We should at least look at it while we're up here," he insisted.

I pulled out the map from the back of the car and we checked out where we ought to go.

Aunt Patty's Lane, off Sunset Hill Road, crossed right over the little brook. We parked at the bridge and I grabbed the rod that I had permanently stowed in the back of the car. Because we were north of the state park, and this land was private, we were a bit wary. Josh and I had been poaching partners for years, and as usual we had our ready-made excuses to combat suspicious landowners, but spending time with Haines had made me extra aware. As we walked into the woods I practiced one on Josh.

"Oh, this is *your* land? I'm so sorry. We were just hiking up through Huntington Park. We must have missed the park border—I hadn't realized it was private here."

The first thing I noticed about the stream was that it was bigger than the small tributary that wound through the hatchery's lawn. The second thing was that it flowed north, which was peculiarly disorienting because most of the streams I'd fished flowed south. Looking into it, I realized that I had been wrong to doubt the man's word. A swarm of little brook trout held in the feeble current, thick as the autumnal leaves that blanketed the brook's bottom.

"Josh!" I whispered harshly. "You see that group of fish in the pool?"

"Are you kidding? There's got to be two dozen of them."

I positioned myself, and casting in the middle of them on my knees, I hooked a miniature trout, about five inches long.

"My God," Josh said as I lifted it out of the water. "That is a beautiful fish."

The trout had a golden belly and blue and red spots. I laid it on the yellow and red sugar and swamp maple leaves, and the colors of the little trout were nicely complemented.

"Get it back in the water," Josh said. I held it in the cool water and let it go, watching it dart under the opposite bank. We had discovered a wild brook-trout stream almost all by ourselves, one that probably no one else fished. As with all good secrets, I yearned to tell someone, though I was determined to try to keep this one to myself. There could be bigger trout downstream! Maybe this was just the beginning and I should keep this brook a secret until I had time to explore the rest of it. But even if I wanted to, who could I tell? Not many people, even fishermen I knew, cared about a trout that was smaller than their hand. And then there was Haines.

Haines was cleaning his shed when I drove by on my way home after dropping Josh off. I stopped to see him, confident that I could keep my new secret.

"I found a wild brook trout stream with Josh, but I don't want to tell anyone where it is," I said, knowing how much he loved to talk, and knowing I would probably eventually tell him where it was anyway.

"Well, James, I told you they're around and that all you've got to do is look," Haines said as he lifted a crab pot and put it on the shelf. His tone bothered me. He made it seem like finding a wild brook trout stream was easy. I knew that if I told him the name of the stream, he would say that he'd fished it, but there could be no possible way that he'd fished this stream before; it was *my* discovery.

"What are you up to?" I asked.

"Oh, Muriel's been after me to clean out the shed, so I'm just trying to organize a bit." Haines was way too good at acting indifferent about my find, so I played along.

"Need any help?"

"Well, just with the engine. We've got to lift it up and put it between the two wood horses like that smaller motor over there." He pointed to the twenty-horsepower prop engine that he wanted me to help him with.

"You grab that side and I'll take it here. Ready?"

"Yeah."

"All right, up; just a bit over. Now set it down." He exhaled. "There, that's good." He paused, took a breath, and looked up into the rafters.

"Were they nice and colored up?" Haines asked.

"Yeah, I guess they're getting ready to spawn."

"Have they got the red bellies on them or are they orangish-yellow type brookies? Or do they live in one of those real stained-black streams, where the brook trout have the black bellies?"

"They've got the orange bellies on them," I said. "The water's pretty dark, but they're not the black-bellied type that you were telling me about."

Haines continued to take things off the floor of the shed and put them on shelves or hang them on nails. There must have been about a dozen big round nets piled in the corner of the shed, and I wondered what kind of fish was big enough not to fall through the holes in the wide woven mesh. Three engines were lined up against the wall. A smoker stood in the corner near the door. Tools of all sorts hung on the walls, tools that could belong to a butcher, a gardener, and a lumberman. Cobwebs covered the nooks by the windows, and fishing rods hung horizontally on the far wall.

"I'd like to show you the stream," I said to Haines.

He looked up and said, "Yeah? If I get Muriel off my back about keeping things in order maybe we could sneak away."

"Well, I'll tell you where it is as long as you don't tell *anyone*."

"You tell me not to tell anyone and I won't tell anyone," he said.

"It's up in Bethel, north of Huntington Park. You know the name of it?"

"Not the Little River, is it?"

"No, where's the Little River?" I asked Haines, realizing that this was probably the best opportunity to get all of Haines's secret spots out of him. Although he had told me a few, I knew he must have some more.

"It's the one that goes into the Saugatuck, by Bob Fort's house. You know where that is, right?"

"Yeah, that white house by the bridge, where the Saugatuck River goes in, right?" I asked.

"Just east of where the Saugatuck comes in."

"And that has wild brookies in it?"

"Yeah, used to be my favorite wild brook trout stream," Haines said. In telling a secret, I had gained a secret. "So what's the name of the brook you're talking about?"

"Wolf Pit Brook," I volunteered under my breath. "That's the stream we discovered today."

"Wolf . . . Pit . . . Brook . . ." Haines said slowly and pensively, as if he were trying to buy time to fabricate a story about when he'd fished it. "I think Bob Chura's fished there," he said finally.

"But it's only three feet wide!" I said defensively.

"Any idea where that name comes from?" I asked Haines. "Wolf Pit Brook?"

Haines walked over to the side of the house in the sun and sat down in a chair. I sat beside him. Nella ran from around the corner of the house and put her head in his lap. An orange-yellow leaf fell from the sugar maples overhead and landed by his feet.

"Well, and this is going back maybe forty years, old Ted Kaechele, not Muriel's father but his cousin, used to tell me that there were wolves around Connecticut a hundred years ago. He said that the farmers used to dig pits and put a calf in the bottom for bait, in order to pit the wolves. The pit was wider at the bottom so that the wolf, when he tried to scramble out, couldn't, and then the farmers would kill them."

"Wow!" I said. "You know, I think I saw a big depression in the ground along the stream, maybe it was one of those old pits."

"Just so you know, old Ted Kaechele also used to tell me that he saw the ghost of a sea captain walking through his back yard."

"Then again," I said, "the hole was probably someone's old dump."

"By the way, doesn't that go through people's yards?" Haines asked, his tone changing just a bit.

He caught me off guard. "Yeah, but I'm sure they wouldn't mind if . . ."

"James, if you're going to fish it, you should get permission."

Just then the telephone rang inside the house, and Muriel came to the door.

"Joe, telephone," she said. Haines looked startled to be caught idle. He went inside, and I followed, sitting down at the kitchen table.

"Hello? . . . Hey, Bobber . . . yeah . . . I got James here . . . yeah . . . Just told me about a native brook trout stream he found."

I was on the edge of my seat. I couldn't believe he would tell, and right in front of me!

"But it's a secret," Haines continued, "No . . . No, it's not on public property. No, James doesn't care." He looked at me and smiled. "He'll go anywhere there's a trout."

If I hadn't known better, I would have almost thought he approved.

Haines skinning Brutus

Brutus

Conroy, holding the .40-caliber Glock handgun, the same kind that Haines has at his side when he's on duty, stuck his hand through the fence, steadied the muzzle against the bull's head, and pulled the trigger. The shot echoed through the silent woods, and the bull heaved and fell over on the hay. Bob opened the gate, and Haines ran in with his knife and jumped on the bull, turned its head, and cut its throat. Rich red blood flowed onto the hay and through the mud. The bull's strong legs kicked, and it gasped and heaved as Haines continued to saw at its throat. It was Charlie Bassman's Scottish Highland bull, named Brutus, which Charlie had bought with the hope that it would mate with the three Scottish Highland cows that were kept in the same pen. But after a year, nothing had happened. Bassman had called Haines with a proposition. If Haines would come over and kill and butcher the bull, Bassman would give him half the meat.

• • •

It was a cold and cloudy November day when I headed over to Haines's house. I parked in the driveway and went in. Haines handed me a plate of sausage with tomato sauce and a fresh roll.

"Here's something to choke the tapeworm," he said. "I don't want you starving out there in the cold."

He walked out of the kitchen and came back with a sheath. He pulled out a knife that had a twenty-inch blade and a six-inch horn handle.

"Here it is," he said.

"What do you use that thing for?" I asked him

"After you shoot the bull, you have to cut its throat to bleed it out. You've got to do it immediately. If you don't, the meat'll be spoiled. Here," he said, "look how sharp it is." He took the blade and ran it over the white hairs on his arm to demonstrate that it was sharp enough to shave with. I took it from him and scraped it lightly over the back of my hand, shaving off a few small hairs.

When my plate was clean, we put on our jackets, got in Haines's truck, and set out for Charlie Bassman's house in the western part of Easton. I had never seen a bull being slaughtered before, and wasn't sure how I would feel. For the moment, I was simply caught up in Haines's excitement.

"Who's going to shoot it?" I asked.

"I think Charlie's daughter, Stephanie, wanted to 'cause it's been mean to her."

"Did it charge her?"

"No, but it's come close."

Butchering a bull was nothing new for Haines. Its death served a purpose; it was going to fill his freezer and feed him for several months. I knew not to bother to ask him if he would feel bad when it was dead.

"When's the last time you killed a cow?" I asked him.

"Two years ago, a few cows escaped from Snow's farm, which is just through the woods behind my house. They came down the hill through the Hydraulic property to my garden and trampled it, destroying practically a whole year's worth of planting. They ruined about a thousand dollars in vegetables, so I said to Farmer Snow, 'You can pay me back by giving me one of your cows.' It was the best deal for him, although he really didn't have a choice. So I went over and took one, shot it, butchered it, and had enough meat for a couple months."

We pulled onto Freeborn Road near the Aspetuck Orchard and then down a dirt road that led back into Hydraulic property. About a mile into the woods, we came to a clearing with make shift fences, a few small shacks, and farm animals.

Charlie Bassman owned a company that installed septic tanks. He had a backhoe and a bulldozer with his name on them parked on the gravel. Haines introduced me to Charlie Bassman and Bassman's daughter, Stephanie, Mike Conroy, and a man who worked for Bassman named Mark. Bob Gost was on his way but hadn't showed up yet. Several chickens and guinea hens were pecking aimlessly around the tires of the truck. One of the pens held several goats and sheep. There was a single horse in the farthest pen, and in the middle pen, behind a shed, were three beautiful, shaggy-haired, golden-colored cows with long sharp-tipped horns. On the ground in front of the three trucks was a huge metal pot with steam coming out, resting on an electric stove that was plugged into a nearby generator. A horrible stench was coming out of the pot. Bassman could see me eyeing it and said, "I got a deer skull I'm boiling in there. Boiling it cleans off the meat so I can hang it up on the shed." He lifted the lid off the cauldron and pulled out the skull of a buck by the antlers. He held it up like a trophy. Even Haines turned from the smell.

"Well, are we ready to get going?" asked Mike Conroy, who was standing back a bit.

"Let's wait another couple minutes to see if Bobber comes by," Haines said.

While we waited for Bob, Charlie Bassman opened the gate to the pen with the three Highland cows in it. To the right was a small area fenced off with heavy steel bars, and inside it was a monster bull, with horns that must have each been three feet long extending from his massive head. His eyes were black and his long fur was a dark musty brown, the color of a black bear's or a buffalo's.

"He must be, what, fifteen hundred pounds?" Haines asked.

" 'Bout that," replied Bassman.

"He looks mean," said Conroy.

"You ever let him out of that pen?" I asked.

"He's been in that small pen there now for three months," Bassman said. "I had him out, just before I put him in here, and he went crazy, breaking down fences. Took me a week to catch him. He didn't run away, just stood in the road there where the trucks are now, and when I'd roll in he'd start snorting and scraping the dirt with his hoof, acting like he was going to charge me. I had to lead him back to the pen with a trail of grain. After that, I knew he had to go, he's been nothing but trouble."

I walked up to the pen and looked at the bull. He was handsome, quite serene for his reputation, though he looked as though he could get mean. A huff of steam came from each nostril and curled like wood smoke in the cold. Charlie took a puff of his cigarette and exhaled.

"You think we should shoot him in here, Joe?" he said.

"Well, I tell ya," said Haines, "sometimes the smell of blood gets the other cows nervous, but as long as you get him out quick after you shoot him, it don't matter."

"Yeah, we'll try to get him out as quick as possible," said Bassman. "We can use the dozer to get him up."

"You should get the other cows out of the pen at least," Haines said.

"I was planning on it," said Bassman. He looked up into the overcast sky, took another drag of his cigarette, and said, exhaling, "So, Joe, you gonna shoot it?"

"I thought Stephanie wanted to do it."

"I changed my mind," she said.

"Well, if I was going to do the job, you should have told me," Haines said. "I would have brought my own gun. Did *you* bring one?" Haines asked Charlie.

"Yeah, I got it."

"How 'bout Conroy?" asked Haines.

"What?" Conroy said.

"Why don't you shoot it?" Haines said, looking at him.

"Sure, I'll do it," Conroy said without even thinking. A small warbler bounced on the ground. It was olive with yellow on the belly and a bluish tail. The bird caught all our attention and momentarily shifted the conversation.

"Isn't it a bit late for warblers to be around?" I asked Haines.

"Yeah, should have been on its way a while ago."

It hopped from cow patty to cow patty, islands in the mud and hay, and under the steel fence where Brutus stood. It hopped on top of his massive hoof and then out again.

"I think it'd be best not to let Brutus out to shoot him," Bassman said, squinting in the cold breeze.

"Man, if that thing went jumping around and broke the fence, this scene would turn into a circus real fast," said Conroy. I knew he was afraid to shoot the bull if it was loose in the bigger pen. "No joke. If he breaks out, this place'll turn into a circus," he said again.

"The only thing I'm worried about," said Haines, "is that if we shoot it in that small pen he'll fall right into that pool of mud and it'll be a real mess when we skin him."

"Well, we can fix that," said Bassman, "we'll just throw some hay down." He walked over to the pile of hay and, grabbing a fork, pitched some into the pen. Haines and Conroy grabbed armfuls of hay and tossed them next to Brutus. Some of the hay landed on his back, but he made no effort to shake it off. Bassman and Stephanie led the three golden Highland cows out of the larger pen and into a smaller one next to it. I walked off into the woods to pee, and the next thing I knew, the three cows were running toward me, their long hair flowing behind them. It was such a bizarre sight that I froze. The cows were followed by Bassman, who carried a whip. They had escaped through a hole in the fence and were running off into the woods. Bassman ran off after them.

"Go ahead and do it without me," he yelled over his shoulder. I returned to the pen and stood near Brutus.

"Bobber's still not here," said Conroy.

"We'll wait a few more minutes," Haines said. "If he doesn't show we'll do it without him."

Haines and Conroy left the pen and Stephanie and I stood with the bull. Brutus stuck his wet nose through the fence to sniff at Stephanie until his long horns knocked against the steel. I hoped he didn't know what was going on.

"Enjoy these last few minutes, Brutus," she said with a hint of regret. Just then Bob Gost rolled into the driveway in his gray pickup.

"Finally," I could hear Haines say as Bob stepped out of the truck. "What took you so long?" I didn't hear the answer. The four men walked into the pen and Stephanie walked out.

"We all ready?" asked Bob.

"Yeah, make sure you don't shoot Bobber by mistake." Haines never missed an opportunity to kid Bob about his weight. Everyone seemed a bit ill at ease to begin with, but Haines's joke didn't seem to help much.

"Where do I hit it, Joe?" asked Mike.

"What we got to do is get his head pointed toward us here," said Haines, "and get his head pointed down."

"That's easy. Just put that bucket of grain over here." Brutus lowered his thick neck to eat.

"O.K., Mike," said Haines, unsheathing his huge knife, "draw an imaginary line between the horns and then one between the eyes—you want to hit it right between those two lines. If you don't get it there, he won't die. That happened to me with Snow's cow. I had to shoot it twice." Bob stood at the fence, ready to open it after the bull was shot, and Haines stood ready to run in with his knife and cut its throat. I stood back about twenty feet. I can't say that I felt bad for Brutus—I had learned from Haines that death was just a part of life—but it would be strange, I knew, to see something living one minute, and dead the next.

A shot echoed through the stillness, and the bull fell on its bed of hay, blood coming out of its nose. After Haines had cut its throat, Mark drove the bulldozer into the pen while Conroy put a chain around the bull's horns. Conroy was still a bit fearful and visibly flinched every time the bull kicked, as if it were going to jump to life and trample him. When Mark had lowered the bucket, Conroy hooked the chain to it. We all stood back and watched the bucket on the dozer lift the fifteen-hundred-pound mass of hair and meat and blood and bone.

"Hope nobody comes driving down here and sees this," said Bob. The spectacle of a bull hanging by its horns from a bulldozer, probably ten feet long, head to hoof, had us all in awe.

Bassman had returned to the pen with the cows and didn't really look toward us. The air was thick with the stench from the pot with the deer skull. We followed the bulldozer with the bull a hundred yards down a dirt road to the woods where the air was clean. A few scattered snowflakes fell. Mark lowered the bull to the ground, where it sprawled on the dead leaves. Bob, Conroy, and Haines set to work with their skinning knives, starting at the legs, making a slit in the thick hide up toward the body. When the legs had been skinned and the hooves lopped off, they tied a rope to each of the hamstrings on the bull's back legs. They disconnected the horns from the bucket on the dozer and tied the ropes at even lengths to the bucket. Mark lifted the bull about four feet and the three skinners set to work. Steaming blood rushed out of the throat, forming rivulets in the leaves. When they'd skinned far enough, Mark would lift the bull another four feet and eventually they skinned the bull all the way to the head. At that point, Bassman showed up.

"There he is," said Haines when he saw Bassman. "Where were you?"

"I didn't really want to watch," he said. "You guys are coming along well, eh?"

"Hey, James, would you pour some of that on my hands?" Conroy asked, pointing to a container of warm water he had brought with him for the occasion. I held it up and opened the spout, washing some of the blood off his hands. Haines didn't stop working, and never washed his hands.

When they'd skinned the bull all the way to the head, Haines opened the belly with his knife, slowly and carefully, so as not to puncture the stomach. The innards spilled from the giant cavity, and when Haines went in with his knife to disconnect the whole mess, he nearly disappeared inside the rib cage.

When the bull was cleaned, Haines cut off the head with a handsaw. The head, the hide, and the guts sat in a great mound, and we turned back toward the pens and the trucks. Haines was careful to remove the heart and liver and carry them back to the truck.

"Boil that skull with them horns on it and you'll have one

hell of a hood ornament for your truck," Haines said jokingly to Bassman.

"I'd need to bring out a bigger pot for that job," said Bassman.

Mark suspended the bull near the shed with the generator, and Conroy pulled out an electric saw and attached it to the power source. They cut the bull lengthwise down the spinal column and lowered it down into the bed of Haines's truck, then cut the halves into quarters at the second rib in from the hind quarter. Tiny bits of bone flew in all directions as the saw did its job, and when they were finished they wiped the meat down with a towel.

Haines walked over to the shed to disconnect the saw, and Bassman, seeing the heart and liver in Haines's pickup, asked Bob, "What's he gonna do with those?"

"He'll eat em," Bob said.

"Yeah," said Conroy. "Joc will eat anything."

We said good-bye to Bassman and headed for the cooler at Slady's apple barn. Since the cooler was owned by his friend Joe Slady, Haines had a key and planned to hang the beef there for two weeks before he butchered it into steaks.

I was in Haines's truck and Gost and Conroy followed in theirs. Haines opened the giant door to the cooler and we walked in to see where the best place to put the beef would be. Immediately, I smelled apples, and looking around, I saw crates about four feet square filled with apples; a different kind in each. There were thousands of them. Haines nodded toward them, indicating to me that I could take one.

I looked from crate to crate with all the different names. I grabbed a Mutsu and a Macoun, putting the Mutsu in the seat of the truck and eating the Macoun, enjoying the crisp, fresh taste. Somehow it felt cleansing after seeing so much blood.

Haines jumped into a little forklift that was used to move crates of apples and drove it up to the tailgate of his truck. They put a platform on its lift and moved the quarters of the bull into the cooler one at a time. The quarters were hung with ropes from two steel pipes that spanned two apple crates. Each quarter, being nearly four feet long, hung just inches from the floor. It had lost all resemblance to anything living, and any sympathy I had for Brutus was gone. The bull had been shot at one o'clock and it was now four-thirty, and growing dark. We said good-bye to Bob and Mike Conroy and returned to Haines's house in silence. I ate my Mutsu apple on the way back.

No one had been in Haines's house since we left. The fire in the woodstove had gone out. Haines threw in some newspaper, some kindling, some logs, a match, and within minutes it was pushing out heat again. I warmed my hands, stiff with cold, until I could feel the blood rushing through them.

Pheasant

PHEASANT

Haines put on a green winter cap, grabbed his gun in its case, and a box of shells.

"What gauge is your gun?" he asked.

"Twelve, I think."

"Well, I'm using a sixteen gauge, but I got twelve-gauge shells. Why don't you go get your gun and we'll have a look," he said.

I went to grab the gun out of my car and handed it to Haines. "An Ithaca featherweight twelve gauge," he said, examining it. "Is this your dad's gun?"

"No, it belonged to my uncle, and my aunt gave it to me when he died three years ago." The gun had a walnut stock and a small etching in the metal of a hunter with his dog.

"It's a good one," Haines pronounced.

We put our guns in the cab with us and Haines handed me an orange vest to wear so that another hunter with a heavy trigger finger wouldn't mistake me for a game bird.

I had told Haines in passing that I wanted cock pheasant feathers for tying flies. It wasn't often that I asked him for things, but shortly he arranged for us to go shooting.

We drove through the quiet town of Easton. I wasn't quite sure where we were headed. Haines eventually turned off on a dirt road, which opened up into a small field of corn, dried and fallen naturally with the season.

"Did they plant that corn for the pheasants?"

"Yup," he said, "for food and for cover, and they also make piles of brush, so the birds have a place to hide. They make cover for the birds and then they go and kick them out of that cover to shoot them." Haines knew as well as I that the hunting club was a bit artificial, but there wasn't much wild game bird hunting left in southwest Connecticut.

We drove on, passed a rundown shed, and then turned off the dirt road into one of the fields. Haines drove the truck over the corn back into the corner of the field. You could hear the stiff stalks that were still standing rattling on the undersides of the truck. A crow flew up in front of the truck.

When we came to the corner of the field, Haines turned the truck to the right and I saw a cock pheasant at the edge of some wild roses by a stone wall.

"Look!" I said to Haines, surprised that he hadn't seen it first.

"All right, that's good. There's one," he said. "All right," he said again, "what I'll do is drive up a hundred yards beyond him . . ."

"And I'll walk around slow and flush him," I said, interrupting.

"That sounds like a good strategy," Haines agreed.

I stepped out of the truck and walked over to Haines's side. He loaded three shells in my gun and put two in his.

"Now put one in the chamber," Haines said, and I cocked the gun. "What you'll want to do is walk up the hill there about a hundred feet, just past that second stone wall, and then walk parallel to the field until you come to the spot where we saw the pheasant. Then walk around that spot and back toward me. When I've seen that you've made it behind the bird, I'll start walking toward you."

"You'll shoot too, right?" I asked. "I'd like us to get him." I knew I was a poor shot.

"Yeah, I'll take a shot," Haines said.

I pushed through the brush at the edge of the field into the woods and walked up to the second stone wall as Haines had instructed. I walked along lichen-covered rocks, and by lichen-covered trees, pale emerald against the brown of the dead leaves. The sun had come out momentarily and briefly warmed me. I was wearing only a sweater and the orange safety vest. When I felt that I had gone far enough, past the spot where I had seen the pheasant, I turned in and started to walk toward Haines, hoping to trap the pheasant between us. I pushed through some heavy brush and a bird went up. When it was sufficiently high that I knew I wouldn't be shooting Haines, I took a shot and missed. The bird continued to ascend, and then I heard a second shot, from Haines's gun, and the pheasant paused in the air, hung suspended, and fell to the ground. Wow, I thought to myself, not bad. Even after I'd spent so much time with Haines, his skills still surprised me.

I looked around a bit and practically right at my feet there was a second pheasant. Walking up to it, I tried to flush it by flailing my arms. It burst up into the air and I pulled, enjoying the sweet burned smell from the shot and the kick from the gun. I missed again. The bird flew up higher, and I took a second shot. Then I heard a third shot and the bird spiraled down and landed in the field. As I was walking out to see Haines, a third bird flew up right in front of him. He lifted up his gun momentarily, and then lowered it down.

"We already got two, James," he said. "Go up by the stone wall where the first one went and I'll get the one in the field."

"They were way up there when you hit them," I said and went to grab the pheasant. It lay on the leaves by the stone wall, an incredible pile of colors. I lifted the bird, still very warm, and turned it in the sun to admire the colors: red and ocher, rust and green. I was sort of glad I'd missed the birds. It was Haines's skill that I enjoyed, and having the opportunity to see the pheasant up close.

The bird swung limp next to me as I walked, a drop of blood encircling its yellow beak. Haines had laid the pheasant he'd retrieved on the dry hay, and I put the one I was carrying beside it.

"Both cocks," Haines said.

"They are a pretty sight," I added.

"You discharge all the shells from your gun?"

"I'm pretty sure I shot them all," I said, and cocked the gun to make sure. I put the gun back in its bag and laid it in the cab of the truck. Haines laid his gun next to mine and started the truck. He put it in gear and said, "Not bad for ten minutes of hunting." We drove back to the main road, not having run into a single person. I got the feeling that I used to get when I poached. There was something about going fishing and no one knowing, catching a bunch of fish, and returning home. It was always that moment when I left the illegal property and first stepped back onto the public road that I savored. Even though Haines was much respected as a woodsman and had permission to hunt and fish at many local clubs, he did not like people to know that he actually took advantage of their offers. He liked to keep a very independent image. In a way, he moved through the woods in secret, too.

We returned to his house and Haines walked inside to put his gun away. I followed him in and sat down at the kitchen table.

"I've got my rifle in the car," I said to Haines, "and was wondering if you could help me sight it in."

"Sure," he said, "but let's clean the birds first. How do you want them done? Should we pluck 'em or just cut the breast meat and the legs?"

"I'm not sure."

"Well, we don't need to pluck them; we'll just skin them and you can make pheasant cutlet and feed your family tonight."

"Don't you want any of it?"

"No, James, my freezer's jam-packed with food. I have three in there already." He grabbed a knife and filled a stainless-steel bowl with water and a good amount of salt.

I followed him outside.

"Why don't you grab the pheasants," he said. We walked over to the picnic table by the side of the house and I laid them on top. He tore the first bird down the belly and exposed the breast. Removing the skin revealed two nice pieces of meat, separated by the breastbone. The feathers folded over one another as the skin began to roll off the bird, which was still warm. Haines skinned around each leg and cut them off, then cut the meat off the breastbone and then the meat off the legs. Each piece that he cut off he dropped into the cold salt water.

"The salt draws out the oil," he said, "and removes some of the gamey taste. But these birds've been raised on corn. They should be just like chicken."

I had decided that instead of taking the whole skin of each bird, I would pluck just the feathers that I needed for fly tying and put them in a bag. I cut off the tail and the two wings and put them in one bag, and filled a second bag with breast and neck feathers. All the time I envisioned the colorful flies I would tie over the winter and the colorful trout I would catch with the flies. We returned inside the house and I watched Haines carefully rinsing the meat.

"Thanks for taking the time to prepare them that way," I said.

"I figured your family would probably want cutlets," he said. "Now, when you get home you can roll these in bread crumbs and throw them in hot olive oil in the pan." He dried his hands and, walking behind the phone, grabbed a paper bag and a marker and started drawing on it. He drew a black dot about three quarters of an inch in diameter and then four concentric circles and then did the same at two other spots on the bag; he was making a target for us to shoot at to sight in my rifle.

"Should I go grab my gun?" I asked.

"Yeah, why don't you."

I stepped outside. It was getting a bit colder now that the sun had gone, but I still wore only my sweater, figuring it might be one of the last days of the season that I could get away with it. I grabbed my shotgun out of the back of his truck, put it in my car, and then picked up my small .22. It was an inexpensive Sears gun that my dad had bought two decades ago. The blue-gray barrel was cold.

Haines came walking out with the target he'd made, Nella jumping around his feet. He started walking up behind his house and I followed, over the still-green grass and under the grand sugar maples to his garden, which stood above the terraced lawn on a plateau.

"I never noticed that before," I said to Haines, pointing to stone walls in a rectangle descending several feet into the ground. "Is that a house foundation?"

"Yeah."

We walked over and stood on it. "There used to be a house here and a barn over there." He pointed to the other side of the garden to another foundation. "They were torn down by the Bridgeport Hydraulic Company when they built the reservoir."

There was an old wooden boat beside a wall near the garden. I'd seen it before but never asked Haines about it. It lay on the ground, mostly just ribs, left like a small beached whale. "How old is that wood boat?"

"Probably been around as long as the reservoir. They used to use it out there on the water." I pictured the old boat on the water with two old men in it, and then I tried to picture the town as it existed before it was covered with water.

———

"That must have been hard," I said as we walked deeper into the woods, "being kicked out from your home and having it torn down to build a reservoir." I had often thought about it while walking through the woods behind my house.

"Well, they came and gave the people fair market value for their homes. They can do it, you know, 'cause they need a reservoir. People need water."

Haines stopped by an old rotting stump, just a bit shorter than himself, which was littered with holes. Putting the paper-bag target against the stump, he took the two nails that were embedded in the stump and posted up the target, driving in the nails with a rock.

"There."

We walked back about thirty paces and jumped a stone wall. Haines gave me three bullets. I loaded them and set the gun on the wall to steady it.

"You know how to shoot a rifle?" Haines asked and then told me, "You squeeze the trigger on a rifle, don't pull it."

I took a deep breath and squeezed, then shot the next two. We walked up to the target. I had shot high and to the left on all three. Haines shot next and did the same, three shots in the northwest, but closer to the bull's-eye. Haines fiddled with the sights a bit and I shot again, a bit closer this time. Haines shot his last three right in the bull's-eye.

"Look there," said Haines as we approached the target, "can't get a pattern much tighter than that." He pulled the target off the stump, and looking up, he pointed at a squirrel. "See that?" Haines said. "That's dinner," and he pretended to shoot it. The squirrel leaped onto an adjacent tree. Nella pounced around the dead leaves and I chased her around the stump.

We walked back down to the house. I took my cutlets home to cook them, the bags of pheasant feathers bulging in my pocket.

Wild turkeys in Haines's yard

LEAD

T he lead was molten; heat waves rose from the top of the pot. Haines took a lead pipe and pushed it into the pot, feeding it in as it melted.

"Now what you do," Haines said, "is wait for it to melt down." He picked up a spoon and skimmed off the dirt that had risen to the surface of the molten lead. The pipe had been a dark slate color, but now was silver. Haines grabbed a mold for fishing weights.

"When you're ready, take the mold and put it under the valve. Then open the valve up and fill the mold with lead." Haines wore a huge pair of fireproof mittens. He opened the valve and liquid metal dripped into the mold. After a few seconds, he opened the mold and knocked the lead fishing weights into a bucket. Winter was the time of year to make sure you had everything you needed when spring came around. In Haines's case, this meant tying flies, ordering lures from catalogs, and

---

making fishing weights from bits of lead he'd collected from various places throughout the year.

Haines left me in the shed with the pot and about two feet of pipe.

"That should keep you busy for a while," Haines said. I was primarily making quarter-ounce split-shot weights for salmon fishing trips to Pulaski. Haines usually made weights for all the people who went on the trip to save them a bit of money. I was also making smaller weights for steelhead fishing in the tributaries of Lake Ontario and big one- to three-ounce weights for flounder fishing in Long Island Sound.

It was cold in the shed, but the pot gave off some heat. Every time the small pot was low, I would take hold of the pipe, wearing the fireproof glove, and push it into the pot until it melted. I tried to keep the pot at least half full. I was happy to be doing something for Haines.

The newly made lead weights were silver and beautiful. With age, they would develop a dark-gray patina. I imagined a shiny weight was more likely to scare away fish. Maybe Haines wanted these to age before he used them.

I sat on a bench hunched over the pot, surrounded by all kinds of Haines's fishing and gardening equipment: nets, engines, waders, traps, a scythe, a hoe, and an ax. Some of the stuff looked pretty old, but then Haines had been around for a while.

When I was down to the last four inches of pipe, I dropped the rest in. I skimmed off the dirt with the spoon as Haines had showed me, and grabbed the mold. There was no recognizable scent from the lead, but I imagined the fumes must be dangerous. I tried not to breathe with my face directly over the pot.

The last of the lead was poured into the mold, but didn't fill it all the way. Only half of the lead weights in the mold came out whole; the rest were incomplete, and would no doubt be melted down this time next year. When I was done, I went inside Haines's house to warm up.

He was at the stove stirring a pot.

"What are you cooking?" I asked him.

"Venison stew," he said, and taking a small bowl he filled it with a ladle and set it with a fork on the table. "Try it," he said. I ate the warm stew with bits of venison meat and cooked vegetables. "How'd you make out with the lead weights?" he asked.

"I melted down all the pipe you gave me," I said. Haines sat down to his own bowl of venison stew at the table opposite me.

"See what's coming now?" Haines asked, looking out the window into the snow-covered woods.

"No," I said, "what?"

"A wild turkey. You watch, more will come out." It took me awhile to see anything except the dark trunks of trees, but then as Haines pointed insistently I saw the first of two dozen wild turkeys come up to the house to eat the corn that Haines put out for them. "There weren't wild turkeys in this area five years ago," Haines said. "They've just recently been making a comeback."

"Seems like they're coming on strong," I said.

"I've seen as many as thirty or forty here at once," Haines said.

The turkeys were beautiful and sleek, even though I couldn't see their colors very well because their iridescence comes to life

127

only in the sun. They were dark and solemn shapes, moving in the snowy landscape. We watched them until dusk and then Haines fed me another bowl of stew.

"I've got some pictures Joey sent me from Colorado," Haines said, referring to his son who'd moved there several years ago. Haines often talked about his son, and I knew he missed him.

"I remember Joey," I said. "He used to cut Mrs. Kaechele's lawn across the street from me. How's he doing out there?"

"Pretty well," Haines said. "He's always sending me reports of the huge trout he gets. Said he was fishing some beaver ponds up in the mountains and lost a six- or seven-pound brook trout. He's caught them up to four pounds in one lake."

Haines pulled pictures out of an envelope. Several of the pictures were of cutthroat and brook trout lying on grass or snow. "Joey said he was fishing the Blue River near his house in Dillon the other day and continued catching trout through a snow squall." One of the photos was of Joey holding a huge brown trout. He looked like a mountain man, wearing a cowboy hat and a belt and holster around his waist with a forty-four-caliber pistol.

"What does he use that thing for?" I asked Haines, pointing to the gun.

"I suppose it's a good idea to carry a gun around. Mostly to scare off bear," he said. "Joey's been out elk hunting recently. He shot one at something crazy like four or five hundred yards away." I could tell Haines was proud of him.

"When I went out to visit in the fall," Haines said, "I caught some real nice kokanee salmon in Dillon Reservoir."

"How big?" I asked.

"A good three pounds. Did I ever show you the video Joey's

friend took of me and him up that small creek with all the brook trout spawning in it?" he asked.

"No, I don't think so," I said. Haines walked into the TV room and pulled out a tape.

"We were up along these beaver ponds," Haines said as the tape played, "and in the small stream that connected them were all these brook trout spawning." I watched the video of a little creek, maybe only two feet wide with barely any water, and all the trout that were trying to spawn in it. Some of the brook trout were exposed completely, stranded on tiny sandbars. Joey and Haines were picking up the trout that had strayed from the center of the brook and putting them back into the water. The brook trout looked to be up to ten inches, with bright red bellies.

"Colorful fish, huh?" Haines said.

"They're incredible," I said. Haines was enjoying my amazement. "Where is that?"

"Somewhere up Copper Mountain, or at least that's what Joey told me," Haines said. The video documented more of the same as they walked up the stream. When it ended I looked out the window and saw snow falling in the headlights of a car passing on the road.

"It's snowing," I said to Haines.

"Yeah, we're supposed to get ten inches tonight. You should think about heading home soon."

"I can't wait to go out for a walk tomorrow in the new snow," I said.

"You should do what I did once," Haines began, "but you can do it much better if there's just an inch or two of fresh snow and not ten inches. I read in *Outdoor Life* when I was a kid that

129

if you start out early in the morning following fresh tracks of a buck, and if you follow them all day, you can catch it."

"Catch a deer?" I asked. "And kill it?"

"Not kill it, but get real close. What the article said was that deer could sprint fast but that they had no endurance, and that by the end of the day you could catch up to a deer." He leaned forward in his chair. "I was in good shape when I was your age. In the army I always finished the races first. It seemed like I could run all day. So I decided I'd try it. The next fresh snow I set out from the house on Seeley Road with a candy bar for energy and started on the track of a good-sized buck. I ran at first and then jogged slow and then walked. All day I went, I never stopped, and by late afternoon I caught sight of the buck. I followed it and followed it until I got right up to it."

"It didn't run?" I asked.

"I guess it didn't have the energy to," Haines said. "I could have probably walked right up and touched it. I suppose that's how the natives used to kill them."

"Well, I'll probably tie flies tomorrow if school is canceled. I don't know if I have the endurance to catch a deer."

"Speaking of tying flies," Haines said, getting up from his chair and putting the video back in its place, "you've got to see the blacknose dace I've been tying." Dace are the little minnows Haines had showed me, and he led me up the stairs to his tying desk where he created flies to imitate them.

"See," he said, picking one out of a box and placing it in my hand. It was made of hair from a buck's tail, three bunches of it in different colors, one tied on top of the other. The top layer was brown, the middle layer black, and the bottom white. "And see here," Haines said, "I painted those little eyes on the head." They were nice little flies. "Here," he said sitting down at his table, "I'll make one for you."

He was hunched over the vise that held the hook in the small, dim room. He turned on the lamp to illuminate his desk. It was piled with feather and hair clippings. He took his thread and wound it on the hook, and then tied some silver tinsel to the body and put that on. After that, he tied on the three layers of bucktail hair: white first, then black, then brown. His hands shook slightly, maybe from running a chain saw, maybe from old age, but he was able to fashion a beautiful and symmetrical fly and paint a small yellow eye with a black pupil on each side of the head. He gave me one of the flies that was already dry.

"Well, James, maybe you'd better head back before the roads get bad for driving."

I put the fly in my pocket, trusting that if it stayed flat I wouldn't get hooked. He opened one of the drawers in his desk and it was filled with colorful feathers. "Why don't you take some of these home with you," he said, pulling out a few of the feathers. I knew he wanted to return the favor of helping him make lead weights. The feathers were beautiful.

"What are they from?" I asked Haines.

"I had a friend who had some parrots, a macaw and some parakeets, and he saved and washed the feathers that fell to the bottom of their cages." The most beautiful one that Haines gave me was a tail feather from a blue macaw.

"See what you can tie with that on your day off from school tomorrow," he said. I left him there, bent over his desk, the lamp lighting his hands as they went to work.

Haines digging for steamers

SHERWOOD ISLAND

Haines always knew the best food to gather at every time of year. He insisted that shellfish tasted better in the winter because they stored up "all the stuff that makes them taste good," whatever that was, and were cold, juicy, and delicious.

Haines decided to go down to Sherwood Island and had asked the night before if I'd like to come along. We had to leave early, because the tide was low at eight in the morning. I had to be by his house at seven-thirty.

"You can get all the mussels you want," he told me, knowing that mussels were my favorite, "and when we get back to the house I'll show you how I make mussels marinara."

It was fifteen degrees when I left my house, cold and quiet and still. It was the day after Christmas.

I'd brought along my dad's clam fork and wore rubber boots, though Haines said we wouldn't wade out into the water. He was primarily after steamer clams and told me to bring a fork if

I wanted to dig for them, too. We drove down through Westport onto the island and across the parking lot where all the summer beachgoers parked. Then we drove across the snow-covered beach. Haines went fast across the sand in his black truck, fearing that if he went too slowly he might get stuck. It had been one of the snowiest Decembers that I could remember, which, granted, wasn't too far back, but Haines confirmed that it was indeed unusual. They were predicting a blizzard for later in the week. When he had driven to the desired spot, a sufficient distance along the beach, Haines stopped the truck and turned off the engine. I put on my wool cap and grabbed one of the two wire baskets that Haines had in the back.

"You're interested in getting mussels, right?" he asked.

"Well, anything really," I said.

"Why don't we pick a bunch of mussels off the rocks first, and then we'll look for steamer clams."

We walked down toward the shore, each with a clam fork and a wire basket. The long silences between us no longer bothered me, and I didn't think it was necessary to always ask questions. The morning sun was surprisingly warm for five days past the winter solstice, but it soon disappeared into a white sky that threatened snow. Haines pitched his fork into the rocks and sand and I did the same. Seagulls scrapped about, looking for a good scavenge. They screeched, reflecting whiter than the sky in the calm surface of the water.

We walked along a slippery area with weed- and barnacle-covered wet rocks. Haines bent over a large clump of mussels.

"Just pick out the biggest ones," he said, "there's more meat in them."

"Like this one?" I asked, pulling one up.

"Yeah, maybe even a bit bigger than that."

The mussels were surprisingly clean of barnacles; large black shells that I knew would give way to plump orange interiors. I picked the mussels like berries and thought about the big mounds of shells they've found from all the shellfish the Indians used to eat. When the bottom of my basket was covered, I noticed that my knuckles were scraped and bleeding from rubbing against mussels and broken pieces of shell. I put on my gloves and continued to pick. The next time I looked up, my basket was half full and Haines had taken up his clam fork and was digging in the sand and rock. He found half a dozen steamer clams and put them on top of the mussels in his basket. My dad called steamers pisser clams. You could find them by looking for their airholes, which they kept open with a stream of salt water that would periodically shoot up a foot or two above the sand.

"How do you dig these up?" I asked Haines.

"You look for their holes," he said, "but you don't dig for them right where you see the holes, 'cause they've got thin shells and the clam fork will go right through them. If you dig to the side," he explained, demonstrating by a new group of holes, "and then ease the fork in, and just let the soil cave into the hole you made, then you won't break them." He did this several inches at a time, caved a layer of sand and rock into the hole, and picked out the steamers as if he were harvesting potatoes. He walked me over to a different spot where he had seen some holes and then went back to unearth some more.

As I began to pile my own store of steamer clams, I pictured them on the half shell or cooked and dipped in butter. The cold always made me hungry.

After I thought I'd got enough steamers, I resumed picking mussels off the rocks. When I next looked up, I saw Haines had staked his fork and had walked to the edge of the water. He was crouched over the smooth, damp sand closest to the salt water, holding a little bag in his hand and dropping bits from his fingers like he was sowing seeds. I left my basket where it was. Intrigued, I walked over to watch him.

"What are you doing?" I asked him.

"Looking for razor clams."

"Is that salt?"

"Yup." He walked along the sand until he saw an oblong hole made by a clam.

Then he took a handful of salt from his bag and sprinkled it into the razor clam's hole.

"Why don't you dig for them?" I asked. "What does salt do?"

"They're too deep to dig for," he said. "Just wait a minute and you'll see what happens." Not very long after he said this, the razor clams started to peek their heads out of their holes. A few came all the way out and were lying on top of the sand.

"Why does salt make them come out of their holes?" I asked Haines.

"I don't know, but it does. Just wait until you taste these— boy, are they sweet."

They were long and thin and curved like the old-style barber's straightedge razors. Haines laid them on top of the steamers in his basket, which was almost full.

"Just one more thing I want to get before we go," Haines said, and he pulled two heavy plastic bags out of his pocket and handed one to me. "These are the plastic bags they put the apples in down at the orchard," Haines said. "They're perfect for oysters."

I hadn't even seen the oysters until Haines pointed them out to me. They were in the same places as the mussels, growing in clumps on the rocks. Haines pulled a few off and, finding an especially large one, walked over to me.

"You know how to open an oyster?" Haines asked.

"No, they don't seem to have an easy way in."

"Well, there's several ways to do it. I like to break off the tip so it's easy to get the knife in. Then you cut the muscles and it opens." He did so with some effort. Given the amount of force he had behind it, if he'd slipped with the knife, it probably would have gone through his hand. But he opened the shell, separated out the meat, and handed me the big oyster, open on the half shell. I slurped it down, along with the icy pool of water it was in; it was cold, salty, and delicious. I was ready for another, but I'd guessed it was time to go home.

We carried our baskets, clam forks, and bags of oysters up the sand and put them in the back of Haines's truck. Haines stopped at the Sherwood Diner. By now it was a little after nine in the morning. We ordered plates of eggs, hash, bacon, and toast.

"I figure we should stop by Red Wagner's this afternoon to bring him some clams. He's getting a little old to be out, and I know how much he enjoys fresh shellfish," Haines said as he sopped up the yolk from his plate with a triangle of toast.

I was satisfied with breakfast, but still could have eaten more. The waitress brought the check and put it between us. I grabbed it and said, "Don't worry, I'll pay for it"

"You don't have to, James."

The waitress, watching the whole thing said, "Let him pay. You've been supporting him all his life." Haines and I looked at each other and laughed. She thought he was my father.

We drove up to the Wagners' house through the snowy streets of the town.

"Red's worked all his life," Haines said as we drove.

"At what?"

"In the sawmill. And his dad worked all his life in the sawmill, too. He'd get up at three in the morning, light his lantern, and walk ten miles to work on the railroad tracks from where he lived in Oxford, to Monroe. And at the end of the day at the mill, he'd light his lantern and walk the ten miles home."

I didn't say anything. We approached his house and drove by the pond in his yard.

"Is there anything in the pond?" I asked.

"Yeah, old Red used to have a lot of trout in it."

"Are there any in there now?" I asked, as we pulled into his driveway.

"I doubt there are any left. The stream that came out of his pond used to have native brook trout in it but there haven't been any there for about twenty years now." We parked and knocked on the door.

An older lady appeared, a bit hunched over, with knitting clutched in her left hand. She pulled the door open and Haines greeted her in a voice more tender than I had ever heard him use before.

"Hi, Betty. We brought you some clams."

"Oh, Joe," she said, "come in." We stepped inside. "And who's this?" she asked, looking at me.

"I've told you about James, haven't I?"

"Oh, yes, yes, now I remember. The boy you caught poaching. Well," she said, looking at me "you and Red can share poaching stories." I smiled and Haines was quiet. It was still a sore subject with him, I guess.

"Come in and sit, please," she said.

Red Wagner was seated in an armchair. His face was ruddy, probably from being out in the cold. On the table next to him was a lamp made out of a mounted yellow-colored trout. Betty Wagner sat in a chair to the left of Red, and Haines and I took the other two seats in the room. The four of us formed a semicircle.

"How've the Christmas tree sales been this year?" Haines asked.

"Pretty good, Joe. Although I don't have many trees left and I don't plan to plant more. Don't have time for all that, got to use the time I got left to go fishing. I see you brought some clams. I been meaning to get out there but somehow the days pass and I don't always get out of the house."

"This is James over here, the boy I've been telling you about," Haines said. It had become apparent to me that most of Haines's friends knew about me, even though I had not met them all. I'd been told by the ones I had met that he'd said many favorable things about me. Old Bill Franklin said, "Yeah, old Joe, he really talks well of you. Says you're on track for a kid your age. He is really impressed with how you tied flies, and he doesn't impress easy."

"Why don't you tell James about the big trout you used to keep in your pond out next to the house," Haines said. Betty Wagner continued to knit quietly. I leaned forward in my chair.

"Well," said old Wagner, "that trout there mounted on the lamp came out of my pond, four-pound golden rainbow trout. Yeah, I had brown trout in there up to about seven pounds and brookies around four. Used to be there was a small dock that I'd feed them off. They would come right up and eat practically out of my hands. Had some perch in there, too. But not like the perch we used to get in the reservoir."

"Which reservoir?" I asked.

"Well, I remember my dad going out fishing through the ice on the Easton Reservoir when I was a kid. Boy, nice yellow perch. And the white perch, you wouldn't believe the white perch we used to get. Some of them went two or two and a half pounds. You ever seen them big perch from the reservoir, Joe?"

"That was a bit before my time," said Haines. The bag of clams in the corner of the room was leaking water, the ice on the shells melting. Haines saw the water and got up to move them. "Let me put those outside." When Haines was out of the room, Red leaned over to me and said, "Some of the best fishing I ever had was in that damn reservoir."

"Me too," I said. Haines came back in and sat down.

"Yeah." Red's voice faded a bit. "My dad used to fish on the ice out on Lake Lillinonah. Seemed there used to be more ice back then cause he used to drive his tractor out onto it."

"Lots of things are changing, all the time," Haines said. "An old farmer used to tell me when I was a kid that when he was young, you could stand at Tashua Church and see Long Island Sound. There just weren't any trees back then. Now you can't see across the street. I would like to have seen it back then." Betty Wagner offered us something to drink.

"That's all right, Betty, we should be heading out."

"Hold on, Joe. I got a battery in the garage for your trolling motor I been meaning to give you. I don't have any use for it, seeing as I have a few extras. It's never been used." It seemed that, just like Haines, old Red needed to give something in return. That was how things worked. I carried the battery to Haines's car.

You could see that Red was thankful for the clams, that he smiled because he knew the smell of steaming shellfish would soon fill his house. But something else was clear: Red didn't quite want to admit that he wasn't in a condition to go out alone to gather them himself. As we left, Red stood in the doorway, waving us off with a grin.

Tip-up on Bantam Lake

ICE FISHING

"Where've you been, James?" Haines asked when I pulled into his driveway at eight minutes to four in the morning. "I was about to call the National Guard to get you out of bed."

"Only seven minutes late," I said, "that's not too bad."

"Well, we'll make Bobber wait just a bit. We taking your car?" Haines asked.

"Yeah, that sounds good, but it might get a bit cramped with Bobber and his stuff in there, too," I said, lifting up Haines's heavy ice-fishing sled and putting it in the trunk.

"Don't forget the bucket. It's full of big minnows for pike. I caught them over at the pond near the parkway. Why don't you fill your bucket with water and take half of them?" I went down to his brook to get some water, and transferred some minnows to my bucket and put both buckets of shiners in the back of the car.

I had been asking Haines for a while now if we might be

able to fish at Bantam Lake, which was a bit over an hour's drive in northern Connecticut. It was the best place in the state to catch a fish that I had only read about—the northern pike, a toothy, long skinny fish with a slate-green and black body, covered with white spots. Haines was reluctant to fish Bantam Lake because the pike were protected and you had to let them go. It was a big deal for Haines to fish primarily for a fish that you had to let go. It made no sense to him, but he gave in. I was grateful that Haines would give up his day off to go to a lake that he had no particular interest in fishing. This favor carried with it a certain obligation, I thought, to at least show enthusiasm, even though it was four in the morning. We were meeting Bob Gost at the diner to get a bite before the long drive.

It was the first time that Haines had been in my car, and it was peculiar to see him there. He looked out of place, not behind the wheel of his truck. "You can move the seat back," I said to Haines, "if you need more room."

"No, it's fine," he said.

We got to the diner by five after four. Gost was parked in the back, sitting in his truck with the engine on, the exhaust piping out, visible under the streetlights.

"About time," Gost said. "We taking that thing?" he said, looking at my small car.

"Yeah," said Haines.

"I don't know if I'm ready to put my life in James's hands just yet. How long you been driving?"

"Since May," I said. Today was January first.

The car really was a bit cramped for three of us and all our gear. Gost got into the back, even though he was about three times the size of Haines.

"Got to let the old man sit in front," Gost said, as he squeezed into the backseat.

"If you weren't such a balloon, you'd be fine," Haines returned good-naturedly.

We drove up Route 25 north, through Newtown and over Currituck Road. My mind began to wander; mornings didn't suit me well, and I suppose I was driving a bit fast.

"Slow down!" Gost said from the back seat.

And a few minutes later, "Stop sign, James. Stop sign!" from Haines. I came to a stop, a bit too abruptly. I could hear the slosh as the minnow bucket turned over in the trunk.

"Oh, geez, James, I think the minnows tipped over," Haines said. I got out and opened the trunk and Haines picked up the shiners one by one and put them back in his bucket, adding enough water from Gost's bucket to keep them alive; all by the light of a flashlight.

"Are you gonna slow down, James?" Haines said to me.

"Yeah, I wasn't really going all that fast, I just stopped too quick."

"Oh well, we're still alive," Gost said.

We drove on, up Route 7 through New Milford. I didn't see the tractor trailer backing out of the supermarket parking lot into the middle of the road. It didn't have its lights on. I heard a *"Look out!"* and felt Haines's hand grab the wheel and turn it sharply to the left.

"What are you doing! James!" said Bob, sincerely shaken up.

"That wasn't really James's fault," said Haines. "That truck didn't have any lights on and was just backing into the road." My mouth was hanging open in shock, my hands tightly gripping the steering wheel. I was surprised that Haines had taken my side.

None of us talked for maybe thirty minutes. Finally, Haines broke the silence. "Your pants wet, Bob?"

Bob's answer was directed at me. "Don't ever scare me like that again, James."

It was getting light when we drove into the town of Litchfield and first caught sight of Bantam Lake. It appeared in pieces through the trees.

"Doesn't look good," Haines said, straining his neck in the passenger seat to look at the tops of the trees. I knew he was talking about the wind. It was blowing fiercely across the ice.

We passed a cove near the road that was filled with ice fishermen, maybe a dozen huddled in twos and threes. Haines had a spot in mind, and that's where we were headed. "Just a bit farther up the road," he said. "There, turn in there."

I parked the car and pulled out my snow suit. I lifted the three sleds out of the car. Haines's and Gost's sleds looked similar; each was a makeshift wooden box on an old pair of sawed-off skis. I'd put all my stuff in a plastic bin that the state gives out to put recyclables in. Usually, if there was snow, they could pull their sleds to the lake, but this day they had to carry them. The snow they had predicted missed this part of the state. Once on the ice the awkward and heavy sleds would glide easily behind us.

We stood at the edge of the ice. About three inches of open water lay between it and us. The ice was new, and new ice is black and hard. But even though it looked as though the solid black ice was a good three or four inches thick, we were careful. I'd noticed Haines had put a thirty-foot-long rope in his sled in case one of us fell through. He was usually well prepared. Since Gost was the heaviest, he was the first one on.

"Bob's the test. If he can stand on it, then it's safe," Haines said.

Bob walked out about thirty feet from shore, took his chisel, and cut a hole. Taking off his right glove and kneeling on the ice, he reached into the water to feel how thick it was.

"It's a good four inches," he called back. I remembered a time we went out on Candlewood Lake on one and a half inches of ice, so four inches made me feel safe.

We walked out side by side, the wind brisk and steady. When we were a hundred yards from shore, Haines decided he would test the ice again just to make sure it was thick enough.

"Here, James, take my sled," he said, handing me the rope and pulling out his ice chisel. He started to rhythmically chop a hole. Just as he was about to break through, a huge gust of wind came and drew the line on his sled taut in my hand and jolted it, turning it over and spilling all of Haines's equipment. My sled had tilted and threatened to flip but remained upright. Haines's bucket of minnows crashed on the ice, sending two dozen fish flopping and freezing. I saw his jigging rod skidding across the lake, along with his lunch. A small plastic container of grubs went bouncing away and three boxes of jigging lures. I stood horrified, not knowing what to do. Should I let go of my sled and pick things up? I could feel my face burning with embarrassment. I handed my sled to Gost and frantically picked up some minnows, my knees soaking up the spilled water from the bucket. I tossed three minnows in Bob's bucket and then retrieved a tip-up and a box of lures. The other equipment was gone, blown out of sight by the wind. I'd never seen such a look on Haines's face before.

"Oh, well, there goes a day of fishing, James," he said angrily, "and a couple hundred dollars of equipment. I ask you to do one thing, and look what happens, you screw it all up."

He wasn't screaming but his tone was harsh. I thought he was out of line, that it wasn't my fault, but I was silent. He seemed flustered, like he didn't know quite what to do either. I was his friend, not his son, but somehow right now we didn't seem to be on equal terms.

"Ease up, Joe," said Bob. "It's not worth getting all worked up about. It *was* a big gust of wind."

"Well, what do we do now?" Haines said, not looking at me.

"We go fishing," said Bob.

"I'll go and look for your stuff," I said to Haines, though I really didn't believe I'd find any of it.

We walked another hundred yards, and then turned to the left, around a small island. I didn't say anything and I didn't look at Haines. I couldn't help but think that if it weren't for me, we wouldn't even be here, and none of this would have happened. I took out my ice augur and began to drill a hole with it. The blades were a bit dull but I got through and set up my first tip-up.

A tip-up is two pieces of wood that cross each other and hold a third strip of wood vertical over a hole in the ice, usually about seven inches in diameter. The reel, attached to the bottom of the vertical piece, is filled with several hundred yards of black Dacron line. When the tip-up is set in the water, the reel is submerged. If the reel were not submerged in the water, then it would freeze when it got wet. The reel is connected to a trigger that has a flag attached to a strip of spring steel. When the reel turns with the weight of a fish, the trigger is released and the flag pops up. Whoever sees it first yells, "Tip up!" or "Flag!"

On the end of the thick Dacron line is tied a section, maybe ten feet or so, of clear plastic monofilament fishing line and then a hook. The size of the hook depends on the size of the fish you are after. About two feet up from the hook, you put two small lead weights on the line to get the live bait down near the bottom. According to Haines, you want the minnow to be a foot or two off the bottom. Haines clipped a weight to the hook and dropped it to the bottom. When the weight hit bottom he pulled the line up two feet, added an extra fourteen inches or so to compensate for the distance that the reel went into the water, and tied a slipknot in the line. Then he pulled a matchbook out of his pocket. Taking a single match, he inserted it through the slip knot and pulled it tight so that the match marked the correct depth. Then he pulled up the line, put a minnow on the hook, and sent it back down to the mark. I watched him do this out of the corner of my eye as I fumbled with my own equipment in the cold.

After I'd set up three, I looped the rope of my sled over a stick that had frozen upright in the water and walked off across the ice to look for Haines's gear. It was maybe half a mile to the other end of the lake. I walked briskly on the ice, sliding a bit here and there. With the sun on my back, I began to heat up. My hat was the first thing to come off, then my gloves, and then my down jacket. I opened my wool coat a bit and felt the cool wind through my sweater. The hair on my head hurt from being twisted and packed under a cap, and I scratched my scalp.

You can't be a more solitary figure than when you are walking across a frozen lake. The solitude did much to mend the event of an hour ago, and I hoped standing still over an open hole in the ice would do wonders to cool Haines off.

The first thing I found was Haines's lunch. He would be very pleased. Then I found his jigging rod with a lure attached to it, one of the two tip-ups that blew away, and one of the two remaining lure boxes. When I got toward shore I saw a white object floating on the few feet of open water between the bank and the ice. It was Haines's styrofoam minnow bucket, but it was out of reach. I thought I'd better look for the more favored items that had been lost. The missing box and tip-up had probably fallen into the water, but it couldn't be too deep because it was so close to shore. I looked and looked in the water, and finally saw a small box three feet down. Taking out the rod I had found, I dropped the lure into the water and hooked the box, hoisting it up. After about an hour away from Haines, Gost, and the tip-ups that I had set up, I felt I should return. I was cold from

150

standing still and put my jacket back on, but quickly shed it when I started walking again. I saw Haines and Gost, two hunched figures in the distance. When I got closer, I could see them sitting on their buckets, their tip-ups scattered out around them.

I walked right up to Haines, who was jigging in one of the holes he'd made. There was another hole about fifteen feet away in which he had one of his tip-ups, and there were three medium-sized perch next to it.

"You got a few already?" I said.

"Yeah. Look, James, I didn't mean to snap at you, but when I ask you to do something you gotta do it."

"I'm sorry," I said and laid the things I had found on the ice next to him.

"I couldn't reach your bucket and one of your tip-ups is missing," I said, "but I got your lunch."

"Thanks. I guess that's the most important thing."

I looked over toward my tip-ups and one of the flags was up, standing tall. I ran over to it. The hole had frozen over with half an inch of ice. I was able to break enough of it with my heel to pull up the tip-up to see if there was anything on it. I grabbed the black Dacron line and pulled it taut. It was heavy with the weight of a fish. I pulled and the line came up wet and limp and I coiled it on the ice, where it froze. The fish had come off. I got another minnow out of my bucket and hooked it through the back, just below the dorsal fin, and sent it down into the dark.

I still had two tip-ups that I hadn't set up, so I swung by my sled and grabbed them and my augur, with my minnow bucket in my other hand. I set up the tip-ups. Although I had ice-fished before I met Haines, I had never used a tip-up until he showed me how they worked.

Nothing happened for a long time. We sat in the cold wind. Then one of Bob's tip-ups went up. "Flag!" Haines yelled. I ran over to see what was on. Bob hoisted a small perch out of the water and dropped it flopping on the ice. It was beautifully colored—bright orange fins and yellow sides, gray-green bars and a black eye. The fish froze immediately, the prickly spines of its dorsal fin poised like bayonets.

I sat on my bucket as the hours passed. I wasn't wearing a watch. The day would be over when I'd eaten the last of the oranges I had brought.

Haines began to pull out his tip-ups and lay them in his sled. I did the same, one by one, and so did Bob. A seagull came down and lifted Bob's small perch into the air and dropped it. As I was walking to my fourth tip-up the flag went up. My walk turned into a run, and when I got to the hole I could see the line zipping off the reel, slanted under the ice with the weight of a good fish. But there was ice over the hole, maybe an inch. It was the only hole I hadn't tended to all day. I banged it with my heel, but I couldn't break it. It was like watching a train I'd missed by thirty seconds leave the platform when the next one wasn't coming for hours.

I looked up and I saw the flag on my fifth and last tip-up fly into the air. Abandoning one for the next, I ran at full speed to get it. The reel was similarly being spooled, the line slanting off at an angle under the ice. I broke the ice with my fist and scooped it away with my hands. Reaching into the icy water, I turned some extra line off the reel and then grabbed the line and slowly lifted up the slack. The fish brought the line tight and I pulled back hard, setting the hook in its mouth. I brought in the line, hand over hand. When its head got near the hole, I reached into the water and grabbed the fish, pulling it up through the ice. Haines and Bob had run over to see it, and I pulled out a tape measure to see how long it was.

"What is it, James, twenty-four?" Gost said.

"No, twenty-six inches" I said, proud.

"Too bad it can't go in the pot," Haines said, as I sent the pike headfirst back into the lake. "But you got your pike and now we can go home."

"Happy New Year," I said to Bob and Haines, smiling.

"If the new year is anything like today," Haines said laughing, "I'm not leaving the couch."

Bob Cost holding two bass

CANDLEWOOD LAKE

I drove down Old Oak Road under a tunnel of large white pine boughs that drooped with the weight of snow. As I passed by Haines's house nothing stirred, not even Nella, who was usually out chasing squirrels after a storm. No one had brushed the new snow from the cars, or plowed the driveway. When I approached the door, I saw footprints in the snow leading to the bird feeder and back to the house. I knocked on the door and I heard a distant, "Come in, James," from the kitchen.

"Weatherman says it's going to be in the fifties today," Haines said.

"Maybe it'll melt all the snow and spring can come."

"This has been one of the longest winters I can remember," Haines said. "I think the sun will do me good." It was already early March and it seemed Haines was ready for spring, too.

Haines gathered his coat and snow suit and we loaded his truck with our gear to go ice fishing at Candlewood Lake. We brushed the snow off the windshield, shoveled out the truck, and left his house.

"We're going to meet Bob, Art Bradshaw and John Resner up at the diner," Haines said.

"Did you hear any reports on the ice?" I asked Haines.

"Yeah, it's still about eighteen to twenty inches thick, but this late in the season you've got to watch out, 'cause even thick ice isn't safe. It starts to honeycomb."

"Honeycomb?"

"That's what they call it, 'cause when the ice breaks apart it looks like honeycombs. This'll probably be the last ice-fishing trip of the year, especially since it's supposed to be so warm today."

"We going up to Sherman Cove?" I asked Haines.

"No, Sunset Cove," Haines said. "We had one day there in March a couple years ago where we did real good for big bass late in the season."

The three other fishermen were waiting in Bob's truck at the diner. Haines took the lead, and the rest of the ride to Candlewood I thought about big bass.

By the time we got to the lake the sun was shining and the glare on the fresh snow that covered the ice was blinding. All five of us toted our sleds across the ice with our rods and tip-ups sticking out of our buckets. Haines brought us to the spot that he had in mind.

"Is this it, Bob?" Haines asked.

"Yeah, I remember it was just off from that blue slide and bunch of cedar trees where Joey got the real big bass," said Bob.

"How big?" I asked Bob.

"Six pounds."

The residents of the lake had all pulled up their docks for the winter and they lay scattered along the shore. We were the only ones on the ice.

Once Haines and Bob mapped out the spot, we started making holes. I had my augur and Haines used an ice chisel. It took us awhile because the ice was close to twenty inches thick. Haines filled my minnow bucket with water from the first hole he made and transferred ten large minnows from his bucket to mine. "If you need more just come over to get them," he said.

We each set up our five tip-ups at a distance of about thirty feet to two hundred yards from shore. Art Bradshaw set his up in a straight line; the rest of us were less systematic. When all were set, there were twenty-five colorful flags dotting the white ice. I sat on my bucket waiting for a fish. The breeze was warm and I took off my coat and put on my sunglasses so my eyes wouldn't strain in the glare. It must have been close to sixty degrees.

The four other fishermen sat silently on their buckets among the tip-ups. After half an hour I noticed that the bucket I was sitting on had sunk into the ice about an inch, a combination of the pressure from my weight and the sun. My ice augur, which was lying flat, had sunk halfway into the ice.

John Resner got the first fish.

"Flag!" Bob yelled, seeing that Resner's flag had gone up. I started running to see what had hit.

"It's a good fish," Resner said when I got to him. "Pulling hard." He was inching the line in with his hands. "Look," he said, "you can see the bottom through the hole. It's only five feet deep here." I knelt down and looked into it. There was a whole other world of green weed and clear frigid water beneath the ice. I looked, and then I saw the fish.

"It's a big bass, a largemouth," I said, "a really good one." Resner pulled it up and onto the ice. I weighed it with the small hand scale. "Three pounds." I'd only caught one bass in my life that was bigger.

I didn't know Resner, but he smiled at me, his huge grin displaying the gap between his two front teeth. We shook hands. "Thanks," he said. "You're Joe's friend?" No one had ever put it that way, but I supposed I was a friend of Haines's. A good friend.

"Yes," I said, looking down at the bass. None of the others had come to watch. "Can I show it to Haines?" I asked him.

"Sure you can, but you'd better get that tip-up first," he said, pointing over my shoulder. One of my flags was up, and I ran over to get it. Resner ran behind me.

"The line's flying off the spool," I said to Resner when we were both at the hole.

"Looks like a big fish," he said. I reached into the water to take the line, and grabbing it, I pulled and set the hook in its jaw.

"It's pulling hard." The fish thumped at the end of the line. It was the hole I'd made farthest from shore, and I'd guessed it was about thirty feet deep where I knelt. When the fish came up, I reached into the water and pulled it to the surface. I measured it at nineteen inches; it was the biggest smallmouth bass I'd ever caught.

I put a fresh minnow on my line, went to get Resner's bass,

and carried both his and mine over to where Haines was kneeling, tending to his tip-ups.

"Look at these!" I said walking up behind Haines.

"Those are good fish," Haines said. "It's just like that day on the ice a few years ago, boy, did we catch some big bass." I noticed Haines wasn't fixing his tip-ups but pulling them out and winding the line.

"You moving them?" I asked him.

"No, I'm packing up," he said. "I'm not feeling too well. Bobber said he'd give you a ride home."

"Do you need help?" I asked him.

"No, James, I'll be all right," he said. I'd never seen Haines leave early from a day of fishing. I figured that he must have been pretty sick. "What you could do," he said, "is make an ice well for those fish."

"An ice well?"

"Yeah, a well to keep the fish alive in. Cut a rectangle in the ice with my chisel, about three feet square and ten inches deep, and then poke a small hole in the corner and it'll fill up with water. Put the fish in there and they'll stay alive till you take them home. Just bring the chisel by when Bobber drops you off at the house to get your car."

I watched Haines finish pulling out his tip-ups. When he'd gathered his things, he walked across the frozen lake, dragging his sled to the other side of the cove where the trucks were parked.

I decided to build the ice well where Haines had been, between Resner and me and Bob and Art. The chisel was sharp and cut the ice cleanly. I started making the general size of the

159

well first, about three feet square, and then made it deeper, cleaning off each layer of chopped ice as I went down. When it was about ten inches deep, I punctured a hole in one of the corners. I tried to make it small, so the fish wouldn't be able to escape. After some time, I hit water, and it bubbled up to fill the well. The well filled up almost immediately. Skimming off the bits of ice that floated on top, I put in the fish.

I crouched down to rest. I would have sat on the ice, but the snow on the surface was quickly melting to slush and I would have been soaked. The bass came to life in the cold water and I watched them swim around, confined.

"Flag!" I heard Art yell, and Bob jumped from his bucket and started running toward the tip-up, his bright orange snow suit bright against the ice.

"Don't come too close, James," he said when I got near him. "I want to land this fish." I think he was still a bit wary of me from his experience in my car a few weeks back.

He grabbed the line and fought the fish. When the fish took the line, he let it, and when it swam toward him, he pulled the line in. I kept my distance. After several minutes he pulled a huge bass from the ice. It was fat, and had a black back, green sides, and a mouth as big and round as a bucket. I'd never seen one so big.

Bob smiled, laid it on the ice, and wiped his glasses on his T-shirt.

"Can I put it in the live well I made?" I asked him.

"Yeah, just don't drop it in a hole on the way," he said.

I had the urge to let it go because it was so big, and old, and deserved to live, but I knew Bob would never talk to me again if I did. When I got to the live well I laid it on the ice and measured and weighed it. It was twenty-three inches and five pounds. I watched it swim around in the well.

The day ended when we ran out of minnows. Between the four of us, we caught twenty bass that ranged from two to five pounds. It was late afternoon when we packed up our stuff. In the reflection of the water in one of the holes I could see that my face was red with sunburn. The tops of my hands were burned, too, and my eyes stung a bit. I don't think I'd ever seen light so bright.

It was tight to get all four of us in Bob's truck, but we managed. The drive back to the diner where Art and Resner were parked took about an hour, which passed mostly in silence. I missed Haines's chatter, and felt a little out of place without him. Bob drove me to Haines's house.

"Don't forget the ice chisel," Bob said when I stepped out of his truck.

"I won't."

"And why don't you bring in two bass for the old man," he added.

"All right," I said. "Thanks again for the ride."

I knocked on the door of Haines's house, and looked through the window toward the kitchen. No one came, but then I heard footsteps coming down the stairs. Haines was in his long underwear. I heard the inner door open, and the outer door rattled from the suction between them and then swung open wide.

"Hi, James, come in. I was just upstairs tying some flies. I figure if I can get a few done a week, then I'll have enough for when spring comes." He looked tired.

———

161

"What do you think you got?" I asked him.

"Just a bit of flu or something. My bones are aching a bit."

"Maybe it's Lyme disease coming back," I said. He'd had Lyme disease in the fall, something a lot of people in town got. It had kept me out of school for three weeks, but was nothing a dose of antibiotics couldn't clear up.

"Yeah, the doctor put me back on tetracycline," Haines said. "Maybe the winter's just getting to me. I tell you, James, every year it gets a bit harder. I don't know if it's age or what."

Haines sat me down at the kitchen table and poured me a cup of warm clam broth.

"You like clam broth, right?" he asked. "My father always used to say that hot clam broth was the best thing for a cold."

I held the mug in my hands and drank the hot salty broth, breathing in the steam and tasting the ocean. Haines sat down across from me.

"I never saw bass as big as the ones we got today," I said. "Bob Gost told me to give you two of them. I put them in the cage in the brook."

"Like I always say, James," said Haines, "every day's a new experience. See that deer out back?" He pointed through the window to where his garden was in the summer.

"No, where?" I asked.

"The dead one on the ground, that brown lump. I picked it up dead on the road and put it there to see what would come eat off it."

"I see it now," I said. "What's come for it?"

"Yesterday evening, before dark, two coyotes were back there chewing at it. One was brown and the other was really dark, almost black. That's the first black coyote I've seen. And they were big. The size of large German shepherds, maybe bigger. And then Muriel was looking out there two days ago, just happened to be looking out the window when she was doing the dishes and called me out of the TV room. A bald eagle had come down, a mature male with a big white head, and started to tear at the deer. Must be the long winter and hunger that gave him the courage to come so close to the house."

"An eagle in your backyard," I said.

"Yeah, that's one of those once in a lifetime things," Haines said. "Every day I go into the woods and never know what I'm gonna see." Haines got up and poured himself a glass of water. It was starting to get dark outside.

"Maybe you should take a bass home with you," Haines said. "I suppose I should be getting to bed, so I can feel better for chopping wood. I didn't think the winter would last this long. But I got enough wood to last a couple more weeks."

I said good-bye to Haines and walked down to the brook. The two bass I'd put in the cage were alive and swimming upright in the current.

I decided to take one of the bass, a largemouth about three pounds, just as Haines had offered. I let it go in the pond at the end of my street.

Haines cleaning trout

EQUINOX

Ifelt privileged to be invited to fish at a private trout club
by Haines's friend Don Halsted. Everything about Halsted
was pleasant. He had a thick head of white hair, and I guessed
he was about seventy—a refined man, but not afraid to get
dirty. Though he was not going to fish, Haines was coming
along to show me where some of the better pools were on the
river and where the trout held. He had fished the club water
several times before, at Halsted's invitation, and knew it well.

I was in the back of the Halsted's Jeep, and Haines was
sitting up front next to him.

"Where are we?" I asked as we passed over a small bridge.
I was thinking that it would be good to come back sometime
and fish the river below the club boundaries, where I wouldn't
have to rely on an invitation.

"Gardner Road," Halsted said, pulling over.

"See that dead grouse in the road, Joe?" Halsted said. "I
haven't seen a grouse around here for years."

"Why don't you jump out and get some feathers for tying flies, James," Haines said. He got out of the Jeep to let me out. I plucked a few breast feathers, took four feathers off each wing, and put them in my fishing vest.

We drove on, continuing down heavily wooded and winding roads, eventually heading up the dirt road that followed the stream. "See those nice deep pools?" Haines said, turning in his seat to look at me. "Those pools hold trout all the time, even during the driest summers. This stream has a good aquifer and lots of food." I looked out the window at the blue-gray water. It was March, the equinox precisely. This was my first trip trout fishing after a long winter.

"I'm going to drive you guys up a bit more and then drop you off. I'll go fishing upstream and drive down to find you around lunchtime."

Haines had suggested that I make a few flies for Mr. Halsted as a gift for the day of fishing. Halsted particularly liked a fly called a muddler minnow, tied with a green wing, and I had tied a half dozen of them in different sizes. Remembering I had them in my pocket, I presented them to him.

"Oh, these are great, James," he said. "I'm sure they'll catch the king trout today."

Halsted stowed away the flies in his shirt pocket.

Haines and I stood on the road as Halsted disappeared in the Jeep. We were both wearing waders and I was wearing my vest, filled with lines and flies and now grouse feathers.

"He put us on a good pool," Haines said. "Why don't you go ahead and rig up your fly rod." I tied on the fly that Haines had given me. It was black with hackle wound around it. The tail and collar were black marabou, dyed underfeathers of a turkey. It was a Joe Haines Special. "Look at it in the water," he said, "see how alive it looks? Just like a real insect."

The Joe Haines Special was, of course, Haines's favorite fly.

The branches overhead were a leafless tangle, but on the twisting strands of thorny wild rose there were little sparks of green emerging. It was the warmest day I could remember since November.

"This stream is full of brook trout," Haines said, "and they're big, fifteen to eighteen inches." The stream was clear, at least where the sunlight hit it. Every pebble on the bottom was visible. In the shade of the bank, the water was black, and I could sense the trout there, waiting.

"There's one," Haines said. "Look." The water flowed and gurgled by, cold and clear. The big spring rains had not yet come, and the air was calm, the dead leaves in the woods dry and brittle. "Look." I looked from where we stood onshore and saw pebbles, and then I saw a branch in the water, and then some larger rocks. "Look," he said, pointing again, "right there, where the viburnum is growing, at the edge of the shade. You can see the fins of the brook trout, the white lines at the edges of their fins." From the pebbles, beneath the glare and reflection of leafless trees, from the branch in the water and the large rocks, materialized a trout. Had it been there before?

"There are probably two dozen trout down there," Haines said, "and now that I've showed you how to cast under the brush and feed your line down in the current you should catch one." I pulled the line off my reel in arm's lengths until it lay coiled on the water.

"Drop it above them," Haines said, "and let it drift downstream so you don't spook them."

I lifted the line and cast it in the air behind me, hooking a tree.

"You're fishing for squirrels again," Haines said. "You don't need to cast it a mile, or even lift the line off the water."

I waded slowly through the stream to the opposite bank in order to retrieve my fly. I moved carefully, the way Haines had showed me; slowly, and without making a wake, all the way to shore. I unhooked my fly from the tree and slowly made my way back to Haines.

"The trout are still there," Haines said.

I let the line out again and rolled it to the opposite bank, giving it time to drift beneath the viburnum.

"There," Haines said. "You've got him!" I pulled back and felt the weight of a large trout on my line.

"Keep the rod tip up," Haines instructed. I hadn't seen the fish hit, but I could tell it was big.

"Take it easy, James. Just lead him away from the others so you can have a chance at the rest of them."

"It's a brook trout," I said. "I've never seen a brookie that big before." It had a wide green back and large light spots on its sides. I could see it spreading its fins, gliding in the water.

"You have a net?" Haines asked.

"No," I said. The trout splashed, and I grabbed it, my hand

barely reaching around its thick body. "Do you want me to keep it?"

"Sure," he said. I walked back up the bank, holding the fish. Haines leaned against a lichen-covered swamp maple. Heat was rising from the leaves below us and I felt the rush of spring.

"These are amazing fish," I said to Haines.

"The big ones are raised at a hatchery in Pennsylvania, but with natural food, so they look wild." The fish that I had caught was about sixteen inches and was the largest brook trout I'd ever seen. It did show some of the wear from being in a hatchery; the fins were not as lacy as on a wild fish. But the colors were intense: a bright red belly, blue and red and yellow spots, and a green back cut with yellowish markings.

I handed the fish to Haines, who put it in the canvas bag slung over his shoulder. I positioned myself and cast again beneath the viburnum.

"I've got another," I said to Haines as I pulled up on a fish. "It's not quite so big as the first." The trout splashed and jumped. It was small, but perfect. I cradled it half in the water and turned it, so the light caught its colors. "I think it's a wild fish," I said to Haines.

"It does look like a native," he said, walking down to the bank.

I unhooked it and watched it dart off. "Are there lots of wild brookies in here?" I asked Haines.

"Yeah, but not just brookies; there are wild brown trout, too."

"You want to give it a try?"

He stepped into the stream and waded toward the center to

position himself for a cast. On the first one he hooked a big brook trout that barreled upstream, almost to the next pool.

"It's a good fish," Haines said. But the trout broke the line.

"I should have tied a new knot after the first two fish," I said to Haines.

He waded up out of the stream. Haines had given me two flies, and now I had only one left. We walked down to where the stream undercut the bank, forming a deep pool.

"There are lots of trout in here," Haines said, "but we'll approach it slow, so we don't scare them off. Just put it against the opposite bank and let it sink a bit." I let out the line. "Not too much," Haines insisted. "Don't take out more line than you need." I let the line out so it would reach the opposite bank, cast it, and hooked a fish about the same size as the first one. "What'd I tell ya?" Haines said.

It came in after fighting a bit, and Haines put it in the canvas bag. The bag was darker now, wet and heavy with the weight of the two fish. I reeled in the fly line and handed the rod to Haines. We continued to catch fish, keeping one here and there, but releasing most of them back into the stream. I could tell that Haines was pleased to be sharing such a great fishing spot with me.

I watched Haines from a soggy part of the bank, skunk cabbage spiraling out of the ground by my feet. He stepped into the stream, water swirling around his legs. He rolled the fly deliberately against the bank, trying different ways of retrieving it, and then set the rod under his right arm to light a cigarette.

Halsted drove up, the wheels of his jeep crunching on the gravel road.

"I see you're doing well," Halsted said, rolling down the window.

"We caught our share," Haines said, releasing another trout he had just hooked.

"Those flies you made for me work great," Halsted said.

"Really?"

"Couldn't keep the fish off that green fly of yours," Halsted said. "And what's more, I lost probably the biggest fish I ever hooked in this river on it."

"This has been some of the best trout fishing I've had," I said.

"Well, James, it's a pleasure to be able to share it with you."

Halsted had kept three fish and between Haines and me we kept seven.

Haines laid the trout on the bank of his brook. He walked to the house and came back with a knife and a board, and cleaned them. I washed the fish off in the water. When he'd finished, we gathered some worms and fed the trout that live in the brook. Haines would never think of eating a fish from his brook. He'd dug out one of the larger pools so it could hold about four seven-inch trout. We tossed the worms in and watched the native brookies zip around the pool to eat them.

Joe Haines's house

ORCHARD

I was heading home down Old Oak Road and saw Haines in front of his house, selecting stones for the wall he was laying. He had been building this wall sporadically now for two years. It was triangular in shape, and when he was done, he planned to fill it with topsoil. Muriel had been on him most every day to finish it, having visions of the flower garden she could plant there. Pulling off the road and parking beside Haines's patrol truck, I got out to watch the slow drama of the selection.

The stones that he had collected were all flat, and piled next to the partially constructed wall. While on duty on the shores of the reservoirs, Haines would pick up an occasional stone and put it in the truck to add to the heap at home. He did not split any stones like a mason, he just used what was there. If he couldn't find a stone to fit, well, that was as good an excuse as

---

any to stop the operation. The next time he was by the shore, he would keep in mind the size he needed. Mostly, the stones were shades of gray-blue or red-brown, shot through with silver flakes of mica.

Haines put a layer of mortar on the previous stone and then placed a stone on top of it, scraping off the excess with a trowel. He put down the trowel to talk with me.

"We've got your favorite for dinner, mussels marinara."

"Sounds good, but I told my dad I'd be home at seven-thirty for dinner."

"Seven-thirty? Well it's hardly six. You can sit down here and have a plate and then head home and eat dinner." I was easily convinced.

We walked into the house and Haines took off his rubber boots, placing them on a mat across from the woodstove. I sat in my usual chair at the round table in the corner of the kitchen, facing a window to the backyard.

Jars of pickled food lined the entire counter in the corner of the room—peppers, cucumbers, onions, and eggs suspended in glass jars. Haines was at the stove, dropping linguine into a pot of water which had just begun to boil. Muriel walked in and sat across from me at the table.

"How's your summer break going?" she asked.

"It's been good," I said, and looked out the window to the green terraced lawn and the darkening wood. "You really have a nice view out here.

"You know, James," said Muriel, "it's one of my dreams to tear down the corner of this house and put in a picture window so I can have a good view of things while I eat dinner." She motioned toward the jars and said, "Right here."

"Muriel, the windows are fine the way they are. This way I can see a woodchuck out in the garden, lift up the window slow, and give him a taste of the old twenty-two. Couldn't do that with a picture window."

"But it would still be nice," she said.

"And you wouldn't have a garden of fresh tomatoes," said Haines.

"Why not?" I asked.

" 'Cause woodchucks eat everything and breed like rabbits."

"Nella does a good enough keeping them away," Muriel replied.

Haines dished out the pasta onto three plates and then put the pot of mussel sauce on the table. The steam from the mussels carried the briny air of Long Island Sound. I ate a first portion and then had a second.

"I like having you over because you have a big appetite," Muriel said. "You remind me of Joey."

Haines interrupted. "Muriel and I are planning on going blueberry picking tonight. If you come, you can fill your gut till you're blue."

"I'd like to come," I said. "Where do you pick them?"

"Up in the orchard."

"Aspetuck?"

"Yeah."

When my dad picked up the phone I told him I wouldn't be home for dinner if that was all right with him, that I was going blueberry picking and that I'd bring home a pint or two.

Muriel cleaned up the dishes and Haines put a bucket in the back of the truck. "Are you ready, Muriel?" asked Haines. She went to put on long sleeves in case the bugs were bad up in the orchard. The three of us hopped into the truck and headed up the road.

As a warden, Haines has special privileges. He held the key to every gate in town, which opened onto miles of trails that wound through the woods. The fire trails were kept clear, their primary purpose to allow access for trucks in case of a forest fire. A secondary purpose for the trails was for patrolmen to traverse the land, looking for poachers.

Aspetuck Orchard is owned and run by the Bridgeport Hydraulic Company. In the fall, the orchard is open for apple picking and people come from all around to fill their baskets. Every inch of the orchard is surrounded by a high, gated fence.

Haines stopped the truck and handed me the key. "Open it up and make sure to close it behind us," said Haines.

"What's the fence for?" I asked as we drove up the hill.

"Keeps out the deer," Haines said. "Deer can jump eleven feet, but not twelve; this fence is twelve feet, so you won't see a deer in here." We were the only ones in the orchard.

"You ever seen a deer jump eleven feet?" I asked as the

truck pulled off the pavement and moved up the rows of apple trees.

"No, but I seen a deer get in Joe Slady's garden and his is nine foot."

The road ended and we got on a path through the apple trees, some small and laden with fruit, others large and sparse. Apples were all around but they were still green and could barely be distinguished from the leaves on the trees.

"Poor peach crop this year," Haines said as we drove through the peach trees. "Not a great bloom this spring." The peaches were just starting to blush with the summer heat. Just another month and their sweet smell would fill the air. "The blueberry crop is tremendous though; they can't pick 'em fast enough."

We had it in mind to make a dent in the blueberries. "I wish you hadn't fed me so much," I said. The bushes stood a bit shorter than me and were heavy with berries. We each went off in separate directions to pick. Usually, more went in my mouth than in the bowl, but there was a slight competitive edge in Haines's eye, and I knew it would become a contest. But after a few minutes of picking and dropping berries in the bowl, I resumed my usual behavior and ate almost all that I picked.

"Wow," I heard Haines call. "Look at all of them over here." He was picking away, loading up his bowl. I would walk up to him and he'd move on. The evening was setting in a bit, and our bowls were filling, even mine. Haines came up to me and tilted his bowl. "Look at those," he said.

"Not bad," I replied and grabbed a handful of his to shove in my mouth. "Yours taste even better than mine," I laughed.

"I might need to borrow your bowl soon," Haines said with a smile, and I poured my berries into his bowl to end the contest. He poured them all into a bucket in the back of the truck.

Muriel had been off picking at her own pace but came toward us. The sun had set and she appeared first only as a dark figure. She walked through the berries toward us with a subtle limp. I realized that her father, old farmer Kaechele, had had the same walk. I barely knew the man, and he had passed away a few years before. I used to see him evenings in the garden, his silhouette against the pond. Mrs. Kaechele was still alive and lived across the street from me in the white farmhouse their family had lived in for generations.

"Let's see what you got," Haines said to Muriel.

"I'm not as serious about it as you, Joe. I like to enjoy myself and eat a few here and there. Actually, I stopped to sit for a while." And then she asked Haines with an almost childlike enthusiasm, "Joe, can we go up the water tower and watch the stars?"

"Aw, you really want to go up there? Then I'm going to have to fetch the ladder and help you climb up and . . ."

It was part of Haines's performance to make you ask more than once. He would always give in to requests, but he liked to make sure that you really wanted it first. And he always enjoyed giving in in the end.

"Please, Joe," Muriel asked again.

"All right."

But there was a kick in his step as we made our way accross the orchard, and he had a slight smile on his face.

The tower was built at the very summit of the orchard, the highest point in town. Constructed like a lifeguard stand for a giant, it was made of wood planks and had a small platform up top. On three sides of the platform there were thick wood walls, open to the sky.

Our destination was visible from the rows of blueberries. Lights from nearby houses began to emerge below the orchard as twilight set in. I hopped in the back of the truck for the short ride to the tower. It was a cool evening, unusual and refreshing for July. Because of the dry air, the stars were not hazed as they usually are in summer, but stood shining in the sky.

I followed Haines to a stand of small apple trees, at the base of which was a ladder. Grabbing each end of the ladder Haines and I leaned it against the tower. We climbed up, Muriel first and myself last.

"This is great," I said. "Thanks for taking me up here. It feels like we own the whole orchard."

"Notice anything?" asked Haines.

"About what?"

"About the orchard, about twilight here?"

"Nothing in particular," I said.

"No deer. Twilight at any other orchard in Connecticut and you'd see them coming up the hill in hordes." I remembered the fence now as I looked to the horizon.

"What city is over there?" Haines asked, pointing southeast to test me.

"Bridgeport?"

"Not bad. You notice that glow from it, the light pollution?"

"Yeah."

"When I was a kid," said Haines, "you could see the Milky Way like chalk on a blackboard. These days, with the cities getting bigger, you can't really see it so well."

My father had already taught me about the stars and all the events in the evening sky. I knew the things that Haines was telling me, but I listened anyway.

Muriel chimed in, "When I was a girl on Kaechele Street in the house across the street from yours, James, you could see twice as many stars as you can today."

"If as many people had disappeared over the years as stars, the world wouldn't be half bad. Everything's overcrowding. Sometimes, I think I won't be able to take it around here anymore with the traffic and the lines, horr-endous!" Haines broke the last word for emphasis. "I waited two hours at the Motor Vehicle Department to pick up my new driver's license the other day. Sometimes I think I should pack up and go to Vermont."

"Or Colorado," said Muriel. "I spent some time out there. Its just gorgeous. And the stars!"

"When did Joey move to Colorado?"

"What's it been Muriel, four years?"

"That long, really? I sure miss him. Good thing we've got you, James." She put her hand on my shoulder.

Joey had moved to Colorado at twenty to become a carpenter. He had recently gotten married to a girl from Texas. The reports from Haines never stopped coming in about the large trout that

Joey was catching out there. I stood between Mr. and Mrs. Haines, looking out into the darkening distance.

Night set in firmly and we descended the ladder with care. We piled into the cab of the truck, and when Haines turned on the headlights, the rows of apple trees jumped out from the darkness.

Holding the carp I kept for Haines

THE GIFT

knew Haines thought baseball was a waste of time, and that
if I stopped by his home on the way back from practice, I
should be prepared for an earful.

"Where were you hot-rodding around this morning?"
Haines asked when I pulled up. He was weeding Muriel's flower
garden.

"I was at baseball practice."

"Baseball doesn't put anything in the pot," Haines said re-
provingly.

"But baseball's fun," I said, a weak defense in his eyes, I
knew.

"Yeah, but what do you get from it? You can't cook a baseball. I could never understand why people hit that ball of rubber
bands around and then go chasing it. Think of all the fish you
could be catching."

Then Haines asked, "How's Whitney doing?" inquiring after a girl I had been dating. He pulled up a dandelion and put

it in a small basket by his knee. "I forget that you're in love," he teased. "Guess you won't be doing much fishing now." He pulled up another clump of dandelions and put them in the basket. "Just let me know when you're ready to sell me your fishing tackle."

"You really think I'd stop fishing for a girl?"

"I've seen it happen before," Haines said. "A guy falls in love, gets married, has kids, and never fishes again. Doesn't have the time anymore."

"It's not like I'm married," I said. "I don't think I'll ever stop fishing."

I had *thought* Haines was weeding his wife's garden when I'd first driven in, but he was actually collecting dandelions, picking them from the hard-packed earth next to his woodpile.

"What are you going to do with those?" I asked him.

"Clean 'em up, throw on some oil and vinegar, and eat 'em," he answered, standing from his crouched position and walking to the door of his house. "What are you up to this afternoon?"

"Taylor and I were going up to Candlewood Lake for trout. Right now, I'm just going to go home, wash up, and put my gear together." My white baseball pants were covered with infield dirt.

"All right, James, just stay out of trouble." He turned and opened the screen door of his house, disappearing behind it.

• • •

Taylor's family had a house on an island in Candlewood Lake. We loaded his boat with our gear at the dock and pushed off around two-thirty. He brought the boat out of Turtle Cove and around the island, headed to another group of islands, dark green humps in the distance. Taylor and I had been fishing the lake for many years. Haines had fished Candlewood most of his life, too, and the spot that we were going was one he suggested. We anchored off one of the islands and began to cast jigs and minnows for trout.

"You want a small minnow or a big one?" I asked Taylor, reaching into the bucket.

"I'll take a small one," said Taylor, which was fine with me because I preferred the big ones. I'd caught my largest trout on big minnows and had grown slightly superstitious. We tossed our lines into the glowing reflection of the sun and sat back to wait.

"What would we do if we didn't go fishing?" I asked Taylor.

"Not a whole lot," he said.

"No, really, what's it like for people who don't fish? What do they do?"

"Needlework," Taylor laughed.

We sat and watched our lines. After a few minutes of silence, I asked, "When's the last time we went fishing for largemouth bass, or smallmouth? Remember when we did that all the time?"

"We haven't done that much lately."

"Haines doesn't fish for largemouth bass. He fishes for trout, and when the streams heat up in June and you can't catch trout, he goes for stripers off the beach. I guess we've been following his schedule the last year or so. Have you noticed that?"

Taylor turned to me with a skeptical look, about to refute this, when his rod jerked and bent over. He jumped up to grab the rod and, with a sweep, set the hook in the fish's jaw. When it came close to the surface, you could see it was a big trout. It pulled off line and went deep again.

"Yahooo!" Taylor yelled.

"Nice fish," I said.

He fought it for several minutes, and when it came close enough I grabbed it by the back and held it in the water. Taylor grabbed the pliers to turn the hook out. The fish must have been a good three pounds.

"You going to keep it?" I asked Taylor. "I wanted to bring a fish back for Haines."

"No, I want to let it go. You can keep what you catch for Haines." And just then my rod doubled over. I lifted it and set the hook, and it pulled just as Taylor's fish had.

"This fish feels bigger than yours," I said to Taylor as I fought it, smiling in friendly competition.

"Yeah, we'll see," he said. I reeled the fish to the boat. We both realized what it was at the same time.

"It's a carp," Taylor said and laughed.

"What's wrong with a carp?" I said defensively.

"It's a trash fish."

"Well, I'm going to bring it to Haines. He eats carp," I said. "He can smoke it or something." Carp weren't exactly known for their table quality. I hoisted it into the boat and cut my line because the carp had swallowed the hook. Grabbing it under the gill I picked it up and admired its green back and big golden scales.

Taylor and I fished until dark, previous chatter having subsided to silence. We pulled up our lines and navigated back to Candlewood Isle by the light of the full moon. It was half past ten when we pulled into the dock. We loaded Taylor's Jeep and headed back to his house.

I drove from Taylor's house along the dark wooded streets of Easton. It was eleven-thirty when I turned onto Haines's road, and all the houses were dark. I walked down to drop the carp in Haines's brook, figuring he would find it in the morning. On my way back to the car, I noticed the light on in the kitchen. Through the window, I could see him sitting at the kitchen table in his underwear and a T-shirt, next to Nella, who was asleep on a beanbag. His white hair, untrimmed, fell across his face. He looked straight ahead and then down at Nella. It was strange to see him so still—not walking through the forest, chopping wood, or cleaning fish. I knocked gently on the door. The calmness on his face changed to surprise and, briefly, fear. He jumped up, ran into the living room and up the stairs, out of sight. I waited at the door and a minute later he came down, wearing a T-shirt and green work pants. He opened the door, turning to show me the handgun he had wedged in his belt.

"Can't be too safe, James. Anyone could come prowling around this house at night. What are you doing here so late?"

"I just came to drop off a fish. I wouldn't have knocked, but I saw the light on in the kitchen and figured you must be up. Sorry I startled you." He smiled when he heard I'd brought him a fish.

"Nella woke me up yelping and I couldn't fall back asleep, so I came down to have a beer to put me out," Haines said.

187

"Want to see the carp I brought you?"

"No, just set it in the brook. I'll clean it tomorrow and eat the cheeks for breakfast. Then I'll smoke the rest of it. Want to come in a minute?"

"Sure," I said. Haines pulled a Genesee beer out of the freezer and a raspberry Shasta out of the fridge for me. He set them down on the kitchen table and put a glass down for each of us.

"I like my beer with ice crystals in it," he said, tilting the glass as he poured the beer. "When are you going to bring me some more bluefish?" he asked. I had brought home blues earlier in the summer.

"Taylor and I plan to fish the sound tomorrow for blues and stripers, out in the islands off Norwalk."

"I've got some big fish there," Haines said, "especially by Goose Island."

"How big?"

"Oh, geez, maybe thirty-five, forty pounds. You know where I used to go every once in a while for real big stripers?"

"Where?"

"To Martha's Vineyard. We'd fish with this guy, name was Captain Bob, using live eels. Put one on the line, bang it on the head a few times to knock it out, and then troll it real slow out over the reefs along shore. Boy, we'd get some real horses. I'm talking forty-five, sometimes fifty pounds."

"Fifty?"

"Yeah, I haven't seen as many big stripers around lately," Haines said as he lit a cigarette. Smoke rolled up to the light and down the cracks in the wood walls. "In all the years I been fishing for bass, I've had least luck on a full moon," he added, commenting on this evening. Nella turned her head and stood up, putting her nose in Haines's lap.

"What do you want, dog? Hey, dog. Look, it's a police dog," he said, lifting the ends of her ears and bringing them up pointy to look like a German shepherd's. "Police dog," he said again and began to stroke her fur gingerly. She wagged her tail and then dropped to her back, legs in the air. Haines stooped down to scratch her belly with his fingernails, sifting through her hair for ticks. He picked one off, a fat, shiny ball of blood that looked like a kernel of corn. It sat on the table between us, along with a few stray dog hairs. I tried not to look at it.

Haines poured the last of the beer into his glass, and I did the same with my soda. "You want me to bring you over some smoked carp?" Haines asked.

"Naw, that's all right. You can eat it all, can't you?"

"Yeah, but maybe I'll bring some over to Joe Slady," Haines said. "He doesn't get out fishing as much as he used to." He took a paper towel, put the tick in it, and then smashed the lump with his fist on the table.

"Well, James, I think I'm about ready to hit the sheets again." Nella was back on the beanbag, her body gently twitching, deep in sleep. "I got up at four-thirty this morning to work in the garden, and if the dog hadn't woke me up I'd be in bed right now. I'll put on the outside light for you."

As we were walking toward the door, Haines put on his slippers to go out with me. I hadn't expected him to leave the house. "I'll come down to the brook with you," he said. The night was warm and I could hear the stream trickling. A piece of the full moon came through the canopy of trees and was reflected in the water and on the large scales of the carp I had brought him. Haines stood beside me in the dark. Once, I might have been uncomfortable in the silence, but now I just saw what Haines saw—the heavy moon in the sky, the softly glowing water, and the flash of the golden fish scales.

"It's a nice fish," Haines said, striking a match to light his cigarette and looking down into the pool. "A very fine fish."

A Note on the Type

This book was set in Garamond 3, a typeface designed by the Parisian type cutter Claude Garamond (1480–1561). This version of Garamond was modeled on a 1592 specimen sheet, which was produced from types thought to have been brought to Frankfurt by Jacques Sabon (d. 1580).

Claude Garamond is one of the most famous designers in printing history. His distinguished romans and italics first appeared in *Opera Ciceronis* around 1544. Garamond's types have been revived in this century, due to their elegant yet clean and open design.